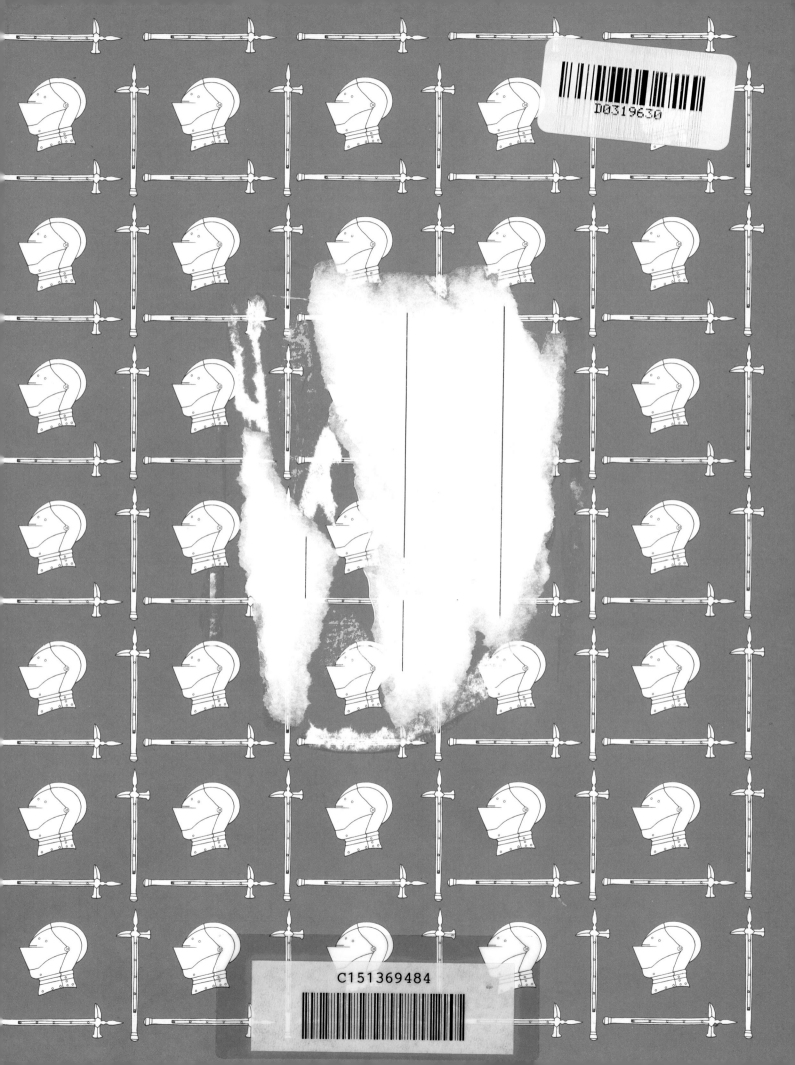

KNIGHT

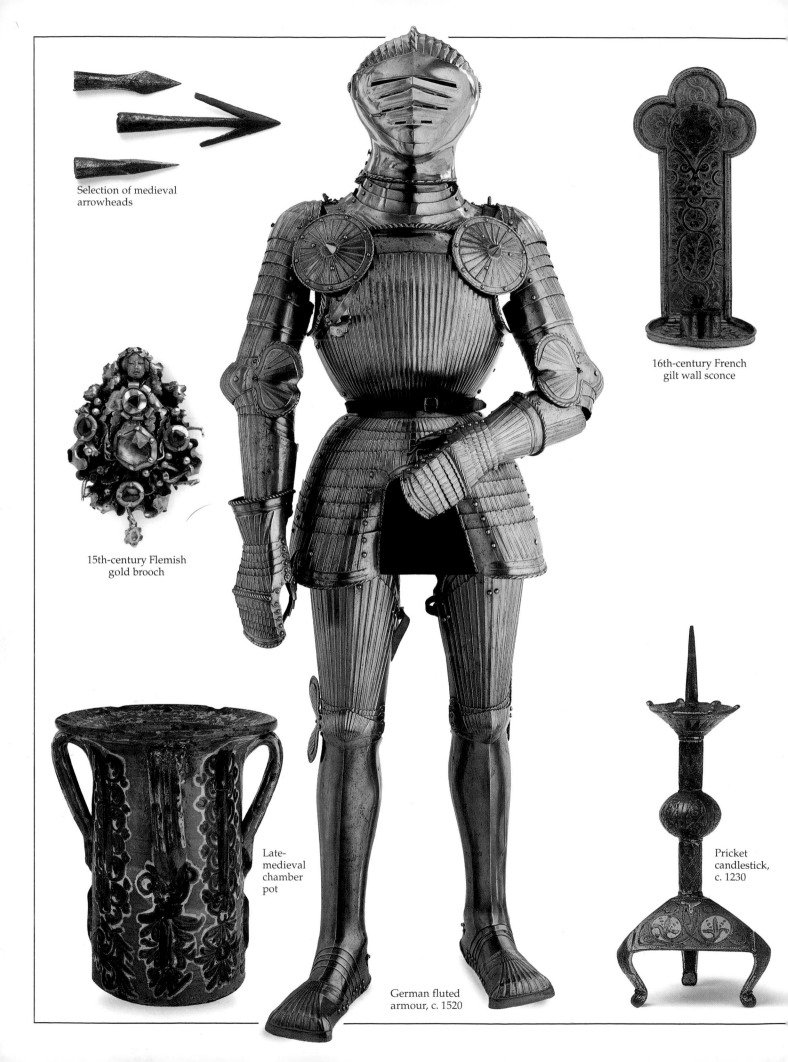

Selection of medieval
arrowheads

16th-century French
gilt wall sconce

15th-century Flemish
gold brooch

Late-
medieval
chamber
pot

German fluted
armour, c. 1520

Pricket
candlestick,
c. 1230

EYEWITNESS ◉ GUIDES

KNIGHT

Written by
CHRISTOPHER GRAVETT

Photographed by
GEOFF DANN

15th-century
German
serving knife

16th-century Italian parade helmet

German
halberd, late
16th century

DK

DORLING KINDERSLEY
London • New York • Stuttgart

15th-century spur

15th-century German shaffron
(armour for horse's head)

DK

A DORLING KINDERSLEY BOOK

Project editor Phil Wilkinson
Art editor Ann Cannings
Managing editor Helen Parker
Managing art editor Julia Harris
Production Louise Barratt
Picture research Kathy Lockley

German
halberd,
c. 1500

This Eyewitness ® Guide has been conceived by
Dorling Kindersley Limited and Editions Gallimard

First published in Great Britain in 1993 by
Dorling Kindersley Limited, 9 Henrietta Street,
London WC2E 8PS

4 6 8 10 9 7 5

Visit us on the World Wide Web at
http://www.dk.com

16th-
century
German
sword

Plaque from a tomb ornament
showing a knight on horseback

394.7 REF

A CIP catalogue record for this book is available
from the British Library

15th-century
Italian barbute

Colour reproduction by Colourscan, Singapore
Printed in China by Toppan Printing Co., (Shenzhen) Ltd.

Contents

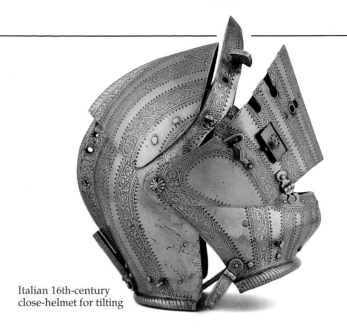

Italian 16th-century
close-helmet for tilting

The first knights

In the fourth century A.D. the Roman Empire fell and Europe was invaded by various barbarian tribes. One of the dominant groups were the Franks of central and western Europe, who gradually expanded their power until, in A.D. 800, their leader Charlemagne became Emperor of the West. Charlemagne and his forebears added to the number of horsemen in their army, giving land to mounted warriors. In the ninth century the empire, torn by civil wars and invasions, broke up. Local powerful lords and their mounted warriors offered protection to peasants, who became their serfs in return. In this feudal system, which first developed in western Europe, the lords themselves owed allegiance to greater lords, and all were bound by oaths of loyalty. All these lords, and some of the men who served them, were knights – warriors who fought on horseback. By the 11th century a new social order was formed by armoured knights, who served a local lord, count, or duke, and were in turn served by serfs.

WINGED SPEAR *right*
Spears with sticking-out lugs were usually carried by the infantrymen (foot soldiers) of Charlemagne (left), but cavalrymen (mounted warriors) might use smaller versions as well. The lugs could stop a weapon sliding down the shaft, or prevent the spear getting stuck in an opponent's body. They might also have helped if the spear was used for fencing.

CAROLINGIAN CAVALRY
Under Charlemagne and his sons (the Carolingians) armoured horsemen became more and more important. In this manuscript of the late ninth century the men have coats of scale armour, helmets, shields, and spears. They now ride with stirrups for a more secure seat. The man in front is carrying a dragon banner shaped like a windsock.

Sharp, double-edged blade

Lug

Socket to insert shaft

BARBARIAN HORSEMAN
When the Roman Empire broke up, many horsemen from eastern Europe arrived in the west. This plaque shows a Lombard horseman of about 600. Unlike a later knight, he uses no stirrups or saddle, but horsemen like him were the forerunners of the mounted warriors of later centuries.

Double-edged blade

Iron crossguard

Flaring blade

Tang of blade, missing its wooden grip

CUTTING EDGE
The double-edged slashing sword was the most highly prized of weapons and the most difficult and expensive to make. At first only wealthy people, such as those with enough money for a warhorse, could afford one, so the sword became the typical weapon of the knight.

BATTLE AXE
The axe with a flaring blade developed in northern Europe. It was especially popular with the Vikings, who fought on foot, but lost favour with European mounted knights. Used by well-drilled infantry, it could prove lethal to horsemen, especially when mounted on a metre-long haft (handle) and swung in both hands.

KINGS AND NOBLES
The king and all his nobles were knights; there were also some knights who were not members of the nobility. In this 10th-century scene the king sits in close conference with his nobles, the men whose armed might kept him on the throne.

AXEHEAD
Many of the tribes living in Europe after the fall of Rome fought on foot and the increase in mounted warfare was gradual. This axehead is from Germany, where feudalism and knighthood were slow in coming.

CHARGE!
Cavalrymen put their opponents to flight in this Italian manuscript of 1028. All the knights wear coats of mail (pp. 12–13) with mail hoods and iron helmets. Straps around the horses' chests and hindquarters hold their saddles in place. These warriors look like tough, practical fighting men rather than the courteous knights of chivalry.

The Normans

IN AN ATTEMPT to stop the Vikings raiding his territory in northern France, King Charles the Simple gave some land to a group of these northern invaders in 911. Their new home was called Normandy (the land of the Northmen), and their leader, Rollo, became its first duke. The Vikings fought on foot, but the Normans, as they became known, copied the French use of mounted knights and became formidable fighters. When King Edward the Confessor of England died in 1066, his cousin, Duke William of Normandy, claimed he had been promised the English throne and invaded with an army. He defeated the new king, Harold, in battle near Hastings and brought the knight, his castle, and the feudal system to England. At about the same time, Norman adventurers invaded parts of southern Italy and Sicily.

SEABORNE ARMY
Grim-faced armoured soldiers with spears and kite-shaped wooden shields stand ready on the deck of a ship. This French manuscript of the 11th century shows vessels like those used by the Normans to bring their invading army to England.

Metal boss

SHIELDED FROM DANGER
This little 12th-century bronze figurine shows that knightly equipment changed only slowly after the Norman Conquest. The top of the helmet is tilted slightly forward, and the figure wears a long undergarment below the mailcoat, on which long sleeves are now common. The shield has a decorative metal boss in the centre.

Prick

Leather straps were originally attached here

PRICK SPUR
This 11th-century prick spur is made from tinned iron. It was fastened to the knight's foot by straps riveted to its arms. Although spurs came to be worn by many different classes, they were always especially associated with knights.

Arm

Position of band to attach strap

Mouthpiece

Double-edged cutting blade

RIDING TO THE ATTACK *above*
This is a scene from the Bayeux Tapestry, an embroidery probably made within 20 years of the Battle of Hastings. It shows Norman knights, who wear mailcoats with hoods and iron helmets with noseguards. They carry kite-shaped shields, swords, and light lances. The small flags, called pennons, on the lances show them to be men of high rank.

SHIELD WALL

In this scene from the Bayeux Tapestry, the English defend their hilltop position at Hastings. Unlike the Normans, the English fought wholly on foot. The armour and weapons of the higher-ranking troops are similar to those of the Normans, except for the large two-handed axe at the shoulder of the left-hand figure. Bundles of javelins and a flying mace can be seen. Norman arrows have stuck in their shields.

SOLID FAITH

The Normans not only used stone to build some of their castles (pp. 22–23), but also built large cathedrals, abbeys, and churches throughout their newly conquered English kingdom. They used the Romanesque style of architecture, which was fashionable in Europe in the 11th and 12th centuries. Typical of the style were massive columns and rounded arches, seen here in the nave of Durham Cathedral.

NOBBLER

This bronze mace may date from the 12th century and is fitted to a modern haft. The moulded nobbly surface could break an opponent's bones under flexible chain mail.

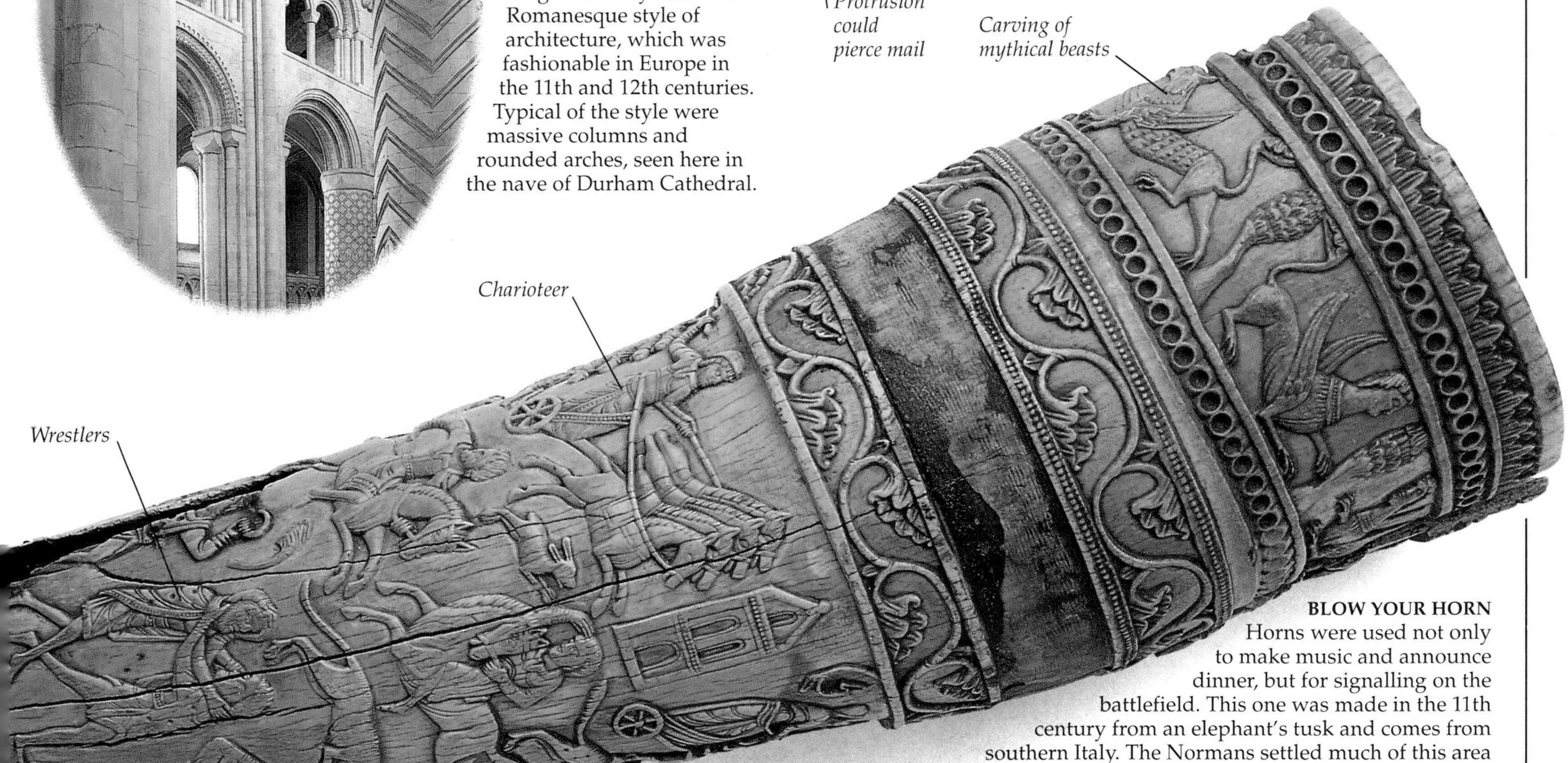

Protrusion could pierce mail

Carving of mythical beasts

Charioteer

Wrestlers

BLOW YOUR HORN

Horns were used not only to make music and announce dinner, but for signalling on the battlefield. This one was made in the 11th century from an elephant's tusk and comes from southern Italy. The Normans settled much of this area and conquered Sicily. The island had a rich mixture of Byzantine and Muslim culture and lay on profitable trade routes across the Mediterranean.

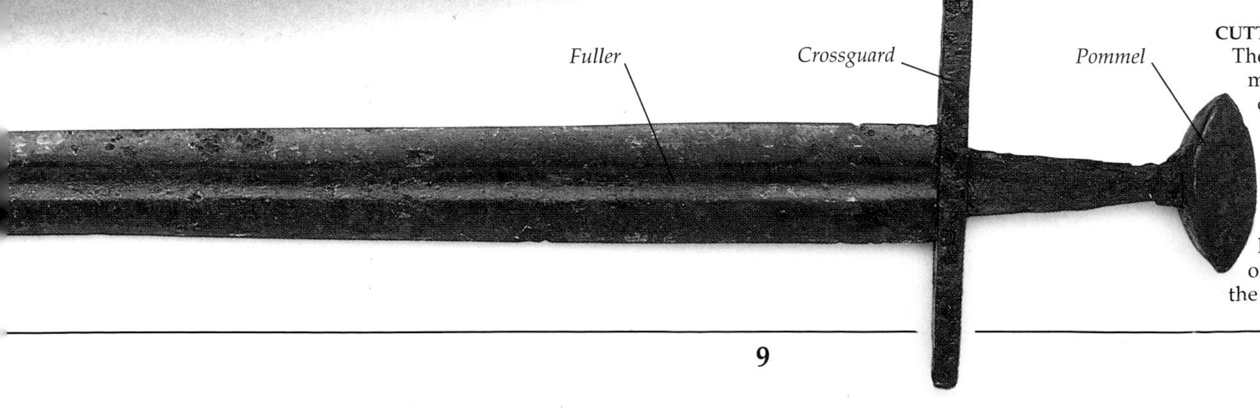

CUTTING EDGE

The sword was the knight's main weapon. This double-edged cutting sword has a groove, called a fuller, running down the blade to make it lighter. The brazil-nut-shaped pommel helps counter the weight of the blade and so make the sword easier to handle.

Fuller   *Crossguard*   *Pommel*

Making a knight

WHEN ABOUT SEVEN YEARS OLD a boy of noble birth who was going to become a knight was usually sent away to a nobleman's household, often that of his uncle or a great lord, to be a page. Here he learned how to behave and how to ride. When about 14 he was apprenticed to a knight whom he served as a squire. He was taught how to handle weapons and how to look after his master's armour and horses, and even went into battle with the knight, helping him to put on his armour and assisting him if he was hurt or unhorsed. He learned how to shoot a bow and to carve meat for food. Successful squires were knighted when they were around 21 years old.

Backplate

Breastplate

BOY'S CUIRASS
These pieces of armour of about 1600 are part of a full armour specially made to fit a boy. Only rich families could afford to give their young sons such a gift.

Holes to attach tassets (thigh pieces)

THE PAGE
Sons of noble families who were sent away at a very early age to the household of a great lord or to the king's court learned a variety of skills. They were trained to serve a knight, to attend noble ladies, and to learn the art of courtly manners and good breeding.

PRACTICE MAKES PERFECT
Young men who wanted to be knights had to keep fit. So squires trained constantly to exercise their muscles and improve their skill with weapons. They practised with each other and also sometimes with their knightly masters, who also needed to keep in trim. Such training was hard and not everyone could manage it. Those who did, eventually went on to become knights. This 15th-century picture shows various ways the young men could train.

Putting the stone

Throwing the javelin

Acrobatics

Fighting with sword and buckler

Fighting with quarterstaff

Wrestling

THE SQUIRE
The word squire comes from the French word *écuyer*, which meant shield-bearer. In the 11th and 12th centuries many squires seem to have been servants of a lower social class, but later the sons of noble families would become squires before being knighted. In the 13th century becoming a knight was so expensive that many young men tried to avoid actually being knighted and remained squires. Later the word squire came to mean a gentleman who owned land.

CHAUCER'S SQUIRE *above*
Geoffrey Chaucer wrote his *Canterbury Tales* in about 1380. One of the stories is told by a squire, who is the lively son of a knight and about 20 years old. He could compose songs, dance, draw, and write. He was also a good rider and knew how to joust. Other stories show that some squires were not as well-mannered as Chaucer's. Sometimes they behaved like thugs. At Boston, England, in 1288, two gangs of squires, pretending to hold a squires' tournament, burnt down half the town.

AT THE PEL
Squires could practise against a wooden post or pel. Sometimes they were given weapons double the weight of those used in battle to help them get used to them and to develop their muscles.

AT THE TABLE
Chaucer notes how the squire carved the meat in front of his father at the dining table. Knowing how to carve properly was a skill taught to these sons of noble families as a part of their training.

Thigh-length leather boots

DUBBING
A squire was finally made into a knight at the ceremony of dubbing. This was originally a blow to the neck with the hand, though by the 13th century this was replaced by a tap with the sword. The knight's sword and spurs were fastened on and celebrations might follow when he could show off his skills. Another knight, often the squire's master or even the king, performed the dubbing.

JOUSTING PRACTICE *above*
This could be done with a wooden structure called a quintain, sometimes shaped like a soldier. After striking the shield at the end of one swinging arm the rider had to pass by quickly to avoid the swinging weight.

Iron, iron, everywhere

THE MAIN BODY ARMOUR worn by early knights was made of mail, consisting of many small, linked iron rings. During the 12th century knights started to wear more mail: their sleeves got longer and mail leggings became popular. A padded garment called an aketon was also worn below the mail to absorb blows. In the 14th century knights increasingly added steel plates to protect their limbs, and the body was often protected further with a coat-of-plates, made of pieces of iron riveted to a cloth covering. By about 1400 some knights wore full suits of plate armour. A suit weighed about 20-25 kg (44-55 lb), and the weight was spread over the body so that a fit man could run, lie down, or mount a horse unaided in his armour. Stories of cranes being used to winch knights into the saddle are pure fantasy. But armour did have one major drawback. The wearer quickly became very hot.

MAIL
In this piece of mail, each open ring is interlinked with four others and closed with a rivet. A mail coat weighed about 9-14 kg (20-31 lb), and most of the weight was taken on the knight's shoulders. As mail was flexible, a heavy blow could cause broken bones or bruising.

KNIGHTLY PLAQUE
This mounted knight of the 14th century has a helm fitted with a crest. This helped to identify him in battle. However, by this time headgear like this was losing popularity in favour of the basinet and visor.

BASINET
This Italian basinet of the late 14th century was originally fitted with a visor that pivoted over the brow. But, probably within the helmet's working life, a side-pivoting visor was fitted. The Germans called this type of helmet a *Hundsgugel* (hound's hood).

MAIL-MAKER
No one knows exactly how mail was made. This 15th-century picture shows an armourer using pliers to join the links. Garments were shaped by increasing or reducing the number of links in each row, rather like a modern knitting pattern.

Pin allowing visor to be removed

Cord allowing mail to be removed

Ventilation holes

Modern mail neck guard

COURTLY GAUNTLETS
Gauntlet plates, like this late 14th-century pair from Milan, Italy, were riveted to the back of a leather glove. Smaller plates were added to protect the fingers. On these plates each cuff has a band of brass on which is written the latin word *AMOR*, love.

SALLET

Light horsemen, who might not wear armour on their lower legs, often wore helmets like this German sallet of 1480-1510. It was originally fitted with a chin strap.

Visor with horizontal sight

THE COMING OF PLATE ARMOUR

The knight on the left dates from about 1340. Over his padded aketon he wears a mail coat and over that a coat-of-plates. His surcoat is short and his legs have some plate armour. The knight on the right dates from about 1420 and has full plate armour.

"Gothic-style" fluted decoration

BARBUTE

Italian barbutes, like this one of about 1445, look rather like ancient Greek Corinthian helmets. The rosette-headed rivets secured a canvas lining band inside, to which was sewn a padded lining. Rivets lower down originally held a leather chin strap to stop the helmet being knocked off.

UNHORSED

Fully mailed knights needed to protect themselves against heavy blows from lances or maces. This picture, drawn by Matthew Paris in the first half of the 13th century, shows the large shields they used. By 1400, thanks to the effectiveness of plate armour, shields had become much smaller.

Pointed cuff

Centre plate

Articulated plates

Shaped knuckle plate

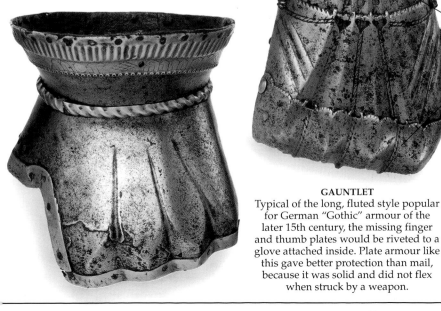

GAUNTLET

Typical of the long, fluted style popular for German "Gothic" armour of the later 15th century, the missing finger and thumb plates would be riveted to a glove attached inside. Plate armour like this gave better protection than mail, because it was solid and did not flex when struck by a weapon.

THE MAILED KNIGHT

This knight of about 1250 wears a cloth surcoat over his mail, perhaps in imitation of Muslim dress seen on crusade (pp.54–55). His mail sleeves are extended into mittens, with leather palms to give a good grip.

Fashion in steel

BY THE 15TH CENTURY, knights were protecting themselves with full suits of plate armour designed to make the edges and points of weapons glance from their smooth surfaces. This reduced the impact of any blows but still allowed the armour to be made reasonably light. Plate armour was often made to imitate civilian fashions. Some armours were partly painted black, both to preserve the metal and as a decoration; or they could be "blued", by controlled heating of the metal. Some pieces were engraved with a pointed tool, and from the 16th century, designs were often etched into the metal with acid. Gold plating, or gilding, was sometimes used to embellish borders or bands of decoration and, in some cases, entire armours.

"Bellows" visor, so-called because of its shape

Shoulder defence made from several articulated (individually moving) plates

Besagew to guard the armpit

Blued, etched and gilt wings

Embossed, etched and gilt dolphin's mask placed over fish-tailed scrolls

OPEN TO THE AIR
The burgonet was an open-faced helmet which allowed more air to reach the face than the close-helmet below. This example, with its decoration imitating the art of ancient Rome, was intended for use in parades rather than for warfare. It was made in Augsburg, Germany, in about 1520.

Burgonet

"Wing" on the poleyn or knee guard protected the wearer from side cuts

PUCKER SUIT
The ridges in this German armour of about 1520 imitate the pleated clothing of the time. The style is called "Maximilian" after the German emperor, although he does not seem to have been connected with it. It combines the rounded Italian style with the German fluted decoration of the 15th century. This form of armour remained popular until about 1530. This suit is made up of surviving pieces from several similar armours of the same period.

Cherubs' head

Visor pivots at the same point as the rest of the faceguard

Peg for lifting visor

PROTECTING THE FACE
A close-helmet is one with a visor to protect the wearer's face. This one was probably made in France in about 1575. It is covered with embossed decoration, which was usually added to armour made for parades.

Figures in Roman armour

Sleeping lion

Close-helmet

Gorget plates attached to the buffe protect the throat

Large pauldrons made of several strips of steel joined internally by leather straps which let them move

Lance-rest helped support the weight of the lance and prevent it being rammed through the armpit on impact

Slim plates on this falling buffe may be lowered over one another to allow more air to reach the face

Reinforcing breast (plackart) attached to the breastplate to increase protection against firearms

Small plates on the gauntlets give complete freedom of movement to the hand

LATEST FASHION
This armour was made for Lord Buckhurst in about 1587. It is a product of the workshops in Greenwich set up by Henry VIII. The breastplate has followed the fashion in becoming more and more pointed at the waist until, as here, the full shape known as a "peascod" is formed. The bulging hips allow for cloth trunk-hose worn beneath. The burgonet has a triple-barred face-guard behind a removable buffe.

Flexible sabaton leaves the sole exposed so the shoe beneath does not skid

Poleyn has plates above and below which allow the knee to bend without exposing the hose beneath

TRIUMPHAL ENTRY
This picture of King Louis XII of France entering Quenes was painted about 1510. The coloured cloth skirts popular at the time were called "bases". The king's helmet is fitted with a heraldic crest.

MASTER DRAWING
Jacob Halder, who was Master Armourer at Greenwich, near London, produced illustrations for people who wanted armour made, often in the form of a set of pieces called a garniture which could be made into armours for war and tournament. This one was for Sir Henry Lee, Master of the Armouries 1578–1610.

ON PARADE
Three knights ride in procession, from the early 16th-century *Triumph of Maximilian*. They carry enormous parade banners representing Styria, Austria, and Old Austria. The horses wear plate armour; the animal in the middle even has pieces to guard his upper legs – such items were very rare.

Armour, the inside story

People often think that plate armour is clumsy and stiff. But if it were, it would be little use on the battlefield. In fact, a man in armour could do just about anything a man can do when not wearing it. The secret lies in the way armourers made the plates so that they could move with each other and with the wearer. Some plates were attached to each other with a rivet, which allowed the two parts to pivot (turn) at that point. Others were joined by a sliding rivet, one part of which was set not in a round hole but in a slot, so the two plates could move in and out. Internal leather connecting straps, called "leathers", also allowed this type of movement. Tubular-shaped plates could also have a sticking-up or flanged edge to fit inside the edge of another tubular plate so that they could twist around.

Key to lock down visor in bevor

Visor

Slot for missing visor-lifting peg

Reinforcing plate

Upper bevor

Hook and eye to hold visor down in bevor

Skull

Trap-door to help breathing

Hinge to fix upper to lower bevor

Lower bevor

Plume holder

Rivet to secure lining

Hinged strap to link lower bevor to skull

CLOSE HELMET FOR THE TILT
This etched North Italian helmet of about 1570 has a reinforcing plate riveted to the skull or bowl. The visor fits inside the bevor, which is divided into upper and lower parts. The visor and the two parts of the bevor all pivot at the same point on each side of the skull and can be locked together.

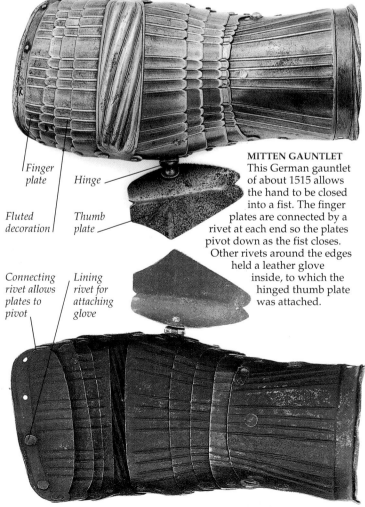

Finger plate

Hinge

Fluted decoration

Thumb plate

MITTEN GAUNTLET
This German gauntlet of about 1515 allows the hand to be closed into a fist. The finger plates are connected by a rivet at each end so the plates pivot down as the fist closes. Other rivets around the edges held a leather glove inside, to which the hinged thumb plate was attached.

HOT WORK
An armourer has heated a piece of metal in a furnace to soften it and is hammering it into shape over an anvil set in a tree trunk. A bellows forces air over the fire to raise the temperature.

Connecting leather (replacement)

Couter

Connecting rivet allows plates to pivot

Lining rivet for attaching glove

Hole for sprung stud on rear plate to close lower cannon

Hinge

Lower cannon of vambrace

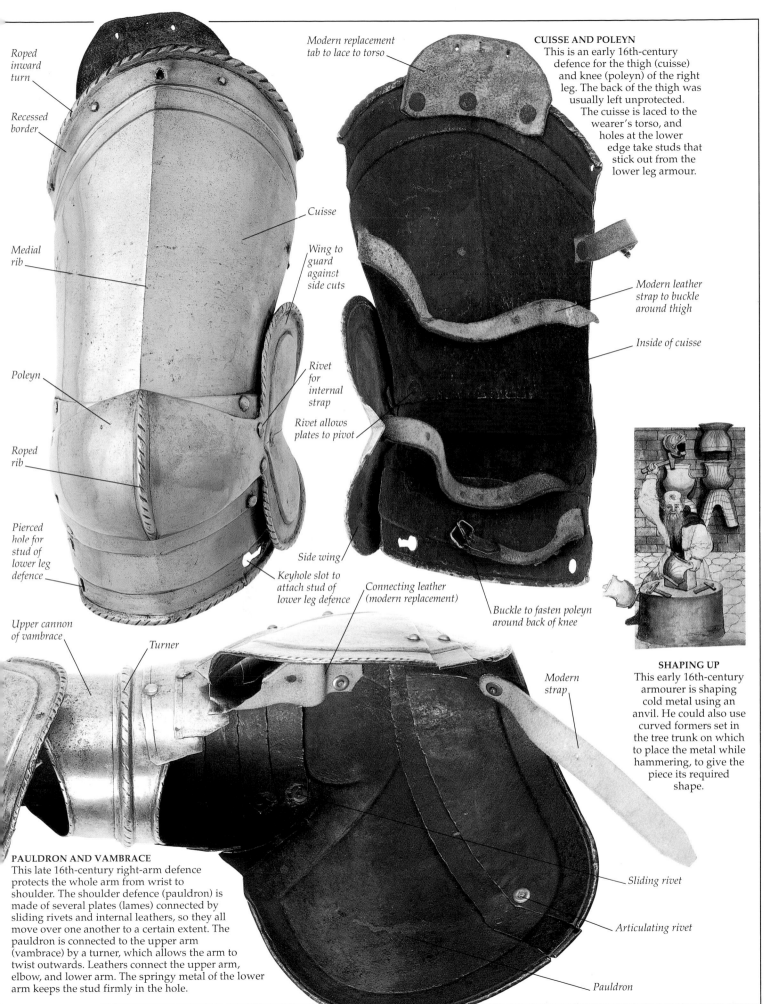

Roped inward turn

Recessed border

Medial rib

Poleyn

Roped rib

Pierced hole for stud of lower leg defence

Cuisse

Wing to guard against side cuts

Rivet for internal strap

Rivet allows plates to pivot

Side wing

Keyhole slot to attach stud of lower leg defence

Modern replacement tab to lace to torso

CUISSE AND POLEYN
This is an early 16th-century defence for the thigh (cuisse) and knee (poleyn) of the right leg. The back of the thigh was usually left unprotected. The cuisse is laced to the wearer's torso, and holes at the lower edge take studs that stick out from the lower leg armour.

Modern leather strap to buckle around thigh

Inside of cuisse

Connecting leather (modern replacement)

Buckle to fasten poleyn around back of knee

SHAPING UP
This early 16th-century armourer is shaping cold metal using an anvil. He could also use curved formers set in the tree trunk on which to place the metal while hammering, to give the piece its required shape.

Upper cannon of vambrace

Turner

Modern strap

Sliding rivet

Articulating rivet

Pauldron

PAULDRON AND VAMBRACE
This late 16th-century right-arm defence protects the whole arm from wrist to shoulder. The shoulder defence (pauldron) is made of several plates (lames) connected by sliding rivets and internal leathers, so they all move over one another to a certain extent. The pauldron is connected to the upper arm (vambrace) by a turner, which allows the arm to twist outwards. Leathers connect the upper arm, elbow, and lower arm. The springy metal of the lower arm keeps the stud firmly in the hole.

Arms and the man

The sword was the most important knightly weapon, a symbol of knighthood itself. Until the late 13th century the double-edged cutting sword was used in battle. But as plate armour became more common more pointed swords became popular, because they were better for thrusting through the gaps between the plates. There was also a rise in popularity of the mace, which could concuss an opponent. Before drawing his sword or using his mace, however, a mounted knight usually charged at his opponent with his lance lowered. Lances increased in length during the medieval period and, from about 1300, began to be fitted with circular vamplates to guard the hand. Other weapons such as the short axe could be used on horseback while long-handled staff weapons, held in both hands, could be used on foot.

AT THE READY
The double-edged cutting sword, shown unsheathed in this 13th-century tomb effigy, could tear mail links apart and drive them into a wound.

THE COUCHED LANCE
Early 14th-century knights charge in formation with lances "couched" under their arms. To keep their line, they rode at a trot before charging as they neared the enemy.

SHINING SWORD
This sword of about 1460 has a copper-gilt crossguard. Like the weapon above it, it was probably made for a rich knight.

Copper-gilt crossguard

Fish-tail pommel　*Horn grip*

CUTTING A PATH *right*
This early 14th-century manuscript shows that double-edged swords were still widely used to slash at an enemy. Surviving skeletons show that the force of a blow could cause terrible injuries and cuts to the bones.

FLANGED MACE
A flanged mace has ridges sticking out from the head to concentrate the force of the blow. Maces like this may have been used as early as the 11th century but became more popular in the 14th century as more plate armour was worn. This example has a bronze head mounted on a modern haft. An iron ball attached to a haft by a chain was called a flail; this was usually used on foot.

Flange

Modern haft

Maker's mark

Fish-tail pommel　*Modern cord grip*

GREAT SWORD
Two-hand swords were large versions of the ordinary sword and were swung in both hands to deliver a powerful blow. This one, possibly made in England, dates to about 1450. Large swords began to become popular in the 13th century and a knight would often hang one from his saddle in addition to his normal sword.

Diamond-section blade

Diamond-profile blade

Crossguard — *Modern cord grip* — *Wheel pommel with cap*

GETTING THE POINT
On this sharply pointed war sword of the second half of the 14th century, the old-style blade with a central groove or fuller has been replaced by a stiffer one with a diamond-shaped profile. This assisted the thrust. The acute point could burst apart the links of a piece of mail.

DEATH OR GLORY
The impact of two riders closing at about 96 km/h (60 mph) made the pointed lance a lethal weapon. In this early 15th-century picture a knight's lance has passed by his opponent's shield and punched through his armour. The figure on the left has a heavy-bladed cutting sword called a falchion. A pollaxe, a staff weapon used on foot, lies on the ground.

WEAPON OF RANK
This sword was probably made for a wealthy person. Dating from the late 15th century, it has a sunken hollow in the pommel which would have held a plaque with the owner's coat-of-arms.

Fig-shaped pommel

Hollow for small shield

SHORT AXE
Knights sometimes wielded two-handed axes, but the smaller, single-handed variety was easier to use on horseback. This 14th-century example, mounted on a modern haft, has the remains of long iron langets which ran down the haft to stop the axehead being cut off. The back is extended to form a beak.

Part of langet

BLOODY BUSINESS
When a dagger was used the opponent was often grasped around the neck before the fatal blow was struck. This often meant stabbing at the face or, as in this late 15th-century example, cutting the throat. Like sharply pointed swords, such daggers could also pierce mail.

Single-edged blade

Remains of gilt decoration — *Rondel*

DAGGER
Knights did not use daggers very much until the 14th century. This is a late 15th-century rondel dagger, so-called because of the protective iron discs at either end of the grip. It was the typical knightly dagger and was carried in a decorated leather sheath.

On horseback

FIT FOR A KING
An early 14th-century miniature shows the king of England on his warhorse. The richly decorated covering or trapper could be used to display heraldic arms and might be padded for extra protection. Some were even made of mail. Notice the "fan" crest.

GREAT HORSE
A destrier or "Great Horse" wears armour on its head, neck and chest, the latter partly covered in decorative cloth. The knight in this 15th-century picture wears long spurs and shows the straight-legged riding position. He uses double reins, one of which is highly decorated.

T HE HORSE was an expensive but vital item of a knight's equipment. Knights needed horses for warfare, hunting, jousting, travelling, and baggage transport. The most costly animal was the destrier or warhorse. This was a stallion about the size of a modern heavy hunter. Its deep chest gave it staying power yet it was also nimble. Knights prized warhorses from Italy, France, and Spain – in fact the Spanish Andalusian is the closest modern breed to the warhorse. By the 13th century knights usually had at least two warhorses, together with other horses for different tasks.

The courser was a swift hunting horse, though this name was sometimes applied to the warhorse, with "destrier" used for the jousting horse. For travelling, knights often used a well-bred, easy-paced mount called a palfrey. Packhorses called sumpter horses were used to carry baggage.

Etched and gilt decoration

Separately moving metal plates

"Eye" for leathers

MINIATURE GOAD
A knight wore spurs on his feet. He used them to urge on his horse. This 12th- or 13th-century prick spur is made of tinned iron. The two leather straps that passed over and under the foot were riveted to the ends of each spur arm.

Prick or goad

Rowel

Tread

ROWEL SPUR *right*
Spurs with a rotating spiked rowel on the end of the arm had replaced prick spurs by the early 14th century. This decorated copper-gilt example dates to the second half of the 15th century.

FIRM SEAT
Iron stirrups like this one dating from the 14th century were worn with long straps so the knight was almost standing in them. This, together with the support of high saddle boards at front and rear, meant he had a very secure seat from which to fight.

Spike with spiral pattern

Brass plume-holder

SWIFT HORSE
A late 15th-century woodcut shows a messenger on his mount. The horse is fast and has enough strength for long-distance travel.

Flanged eye-guard

Nose-guard

NOBLE HEAD
Horse armour was expensive and uncommon. If a knight could only afford part of the armour, he would usually choose the shaffron, the piece for the head. The shaffron probably came into use during the 12th century. This one, complete with crinet to protect the neck, is northern Italian and dates from about 1570. Both pieces are decorated with etched and gilt bands depicting animals, birds, and figures. The crinet flexes on sliding rivets and internal leathers.

15TH-CENTURY JOUSTER
Destrier – from the Latin *dextra*, (right) – may suggest the horse was led with the right hand, or that he led with the right leg so that if he swerved he would move away from an opponent.

Chain goes under horse's throat

Decorated metal boss

Poll plate

FROM THE HORSE'S MOUTH
Curb bits similar to this one were used by military riders from the later Middle Ages to the 19th century. Leverage from the long arms put pressure on the horse's mouth and gave good control.

Ring for rein

MUZZLE
A steel frame is decorated with openwork panels and chiselled bars. At the top, a German inscription reads "As God wills, so is my aim." Below is a crowned Imperial eagle and the date 1561. Two lizards support the panel. The letters at the bottom probably indicate the owner's name.

SHAFFRON *right*
This German shaffron from the 1460s has a poll plate, attached by a brass hinge, to protect the top of the horse's head. The central spike and rondel are missing. The rivets originally held an internal lining.

The castle

A CASTLE COULD BE a lord's private residence or home, his business headquarters, as well as a base for his soldiers. The first castles probably appeared in northwestern France in the ninth century, because of civil wars and Viking attacks. Although some early castles were built of stone, many consisted of earthworks and timber walls. But slowly knights began to use stone (and later brick) to build their castles, because it was stronger and more fire-resistant. In the late 15th century, more settled societies, demands for comfort, and the increasing use of powerful cannon meant that castles became less important. Some of their military roles were taken over by forts, defended gun-platforms controlled by the state.

NARROW SLIT
Windows near the ground were made very small to guard against enemy missiles or soldiers climbing through. Such windows were narrow on the outside but splayed on the inside to let in as much light as possible.

MOTTE AND BAILEY
The castles of the 10th to 12th centuries usually consisted of a ditch and rampart with wooden fences. From the 11th century many were also given a mound called a motte, a last line of defence with a wooden tower on top. The courtyard or bailey below it held all the domestic buildings.

STRENGTH IN STONE
The stone donjon, or keep, became common in the late 11th and 12th centuries. The larger ones could hold accommodation for the lord and his household. The bailey was by now often surrounded by stone walls with square towers. Round towers appeared in the 12th century.

MEN AT WORK
Stone castles cost a fortune to build and could take years to complete. The lord and the master mason chose a strong site and plan. Stone had to be brought in specially. In addition, large amounts of lime, sand, and water were needed for the mortar. The materials and workforce were normally provided by the lord.

RINGS OF DEFENCE
Concentric castles, which were first built in the 13th century, had two rings of walls, one within the other. This gave two lines of defence. The inner ring was often higher to give archers a clear field of fire. Some old castles with keeps had outer rings added later, which gave yet another line of defence. Sometimes rivers were used to give broad water defences.

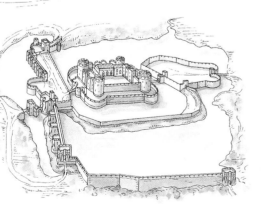

CRACKING CASTLE
Sometimes wooden fences on the motte were replaced by stone walls, forming a shell keep. Occasionally a stone tower was built on a motte, but the artificial mound was not always strong enough to take the weight. The 13th-century Clifford's Tower in York, England, has cracked as a result.

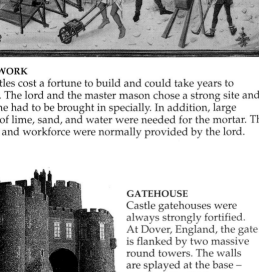

GATEHOUSE
Castle gatehouses were always strongly fortified. At Dover, England, the gate is flanked by two massive round towers. The walls are splayed at the base – the thicker masonry helps to protect them against mining. There is also a deep dry ditch to obstruct attackers.

INSIDE A KEEP
A large keep like the one at Rochester had enough space to house the lord and his retinue. The basement was used for storage. The first floor usually housed the garrison. The hall on the next floor was used by everyone to eat and in some cases sleep in. The lord's family had rooms on the top floor of the keep.

Wooden hoarding to allow soldiers to overlook the base of the wall

Chapel

Spiral stone stairs

Lord's apartments

Great hall

Guardrooms

Storerooms

GOOD SITE
This view of the keep at Rochester shows how it is surrounded by strong outer defensive walls.

A GREAT TOWER
The keep, or donjon (from which comes the English word dungeon, an underground prison), always had strong walls. At Rochester, begun in 1087, they are 3.7 m (12 ft) thick at the base and the tower is 21 m (70 ft) high. The entrance was always on the first floor and was often protected by a forebuilding. There was a well in the basement, to provide water if the garrison was trapped in the tower during a siege.

Merlon or battlement

Corner turret

Buttress to strengthen wall

Large upper window further enlarged later on

Merlon on forebuilding

Chapel window

Forebuilding with entrance doorway

Narrow slit on lower level, to protect against enemy missiles

Drawbridge pit

23

The castle at war

CASTLES WERE BUILT as defences against enemy attacks. The first obstacle for the enemy was a ditch all the way around the castle, which was sometimes filled with stakes to slow a man down and make him an easy target. Moats – ditches that were often filled with water – were less common: they put off attackers from burrowing under the walls. Towers jutted out from the walls so that defending archers could shoot along the walls to repel any attackers. Small gates allowed the defenders to rush out and surprise the enemy. The castle was also used as a base from which knights rode out to fight an enemy or ravage his lands.

Iron-clad wooden portcullis

Wooden doors barred from behind

GATEHOUSE
The gatehouse was always strongly defended as it was thought to be a weak spot. Usually a wooden lifting bridge spanned the ditch and an iron gate called a portcullis could be lowered to form a barrier.

VAULTED CEILING
There are holes built into the stone vaulted ceiling of the castle gatehouse. These allowed people on the floor above to pour water down to put out fires or possibly to drop stones or boiling water on to the heads of attackers.

High turrets gave distinct views of approaching enemies

Gap (or crenel), through which defenders could shoot

Merlon to protect defenders against missiles

Machicolations along gate tower

Battlement on section of curtain wall

Round flanking tower; the shape leaves no corners for a ram or miners

Moat

OVER THE WALLS

This early 14th-century picture shows the 11th-century crusader, Godfrey of Bouillon, attacking fortifications. His men are using scaling ladders, which was always dangerous because the defenders would try to push them away. Archers provide covering fire.

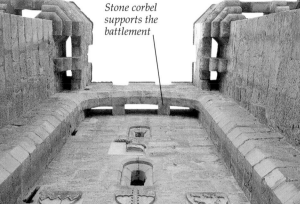

FLANKING TOWERS

This picture was taken looking up the front of the castle. Flanking towers jut out on either side to protect the gate. The battlements are thrust forward (machicolated) so that they overhang the walls. Offensive materials like boiling water or hot sand could be poured through the holes on to the attackers below. The holes could also be used to pour cold water, to put out fires.

Stone corbel supports the battlement

EMBRASURE

An embrasure was an alcove in the thickness of the wall, with a narrow opening, or "loophole", to the outside. This allowed defenders to look and shoot out without showing themselves. In this example, the rounded lower part of the loophole is designed for guns, used more and more in warfare by the time this castle was built.

AT SIEGE

Both the attackers and the defenders of this castle are using siege engines (pp. 26–27) to hurl missiles at each other.

KNIGHTLY STRONGHOLD

Bodiam Castle in Sussex, England, was built in 1385 by Sir Edward Dalyngrigge amid fears of a French invasion. It has a single stone curtain wall with round towers at the corners and is surrounded by a broad moat to protect the occupants. To guard against possible treachery amongst the defending soldiers, there are no connecting doors between their quarters and those of the lord.

Turret or watchtower

Lancet window to let in light but keep out missiles

Siege warfare

Counterpoise arm

Sling

Weighted box

AN ENEMY ATTACKING a castle would make a formal demand for the people inside to surrender. If this was rejected, they would try to take the castle by siege. There were two methods. The first was to surround the castle and prevent anyone leaving or going in, thereby starving the defenders into submission. The second was to use force. One way was to tunnel under the wall and come up inside, or undermine the wall and bring it down. Alternatively, the attackers could try to break the walls down with battering rams, catapults, or, from the 14th century on, cannon. They could also try to get over the wall using scaling ladders or a moving tower fitted with a drawbridge that could be let down on the top of the wall.

Sling pouch

Rope to pull arm down again

TREBUCHET
The trebuchet was first used in Europe in the 12th century. It worked on the principle of counterpoise – there was a pivoting wooden arm with a heavy weight at one end and a sling, containing a missile such as a stone, at the other. As the weight dropped down, the sling flew up, launching the missile toward the castle. Some trebuchets had arms about 18 m (60 ft) long. On average they could probably hurl stones of about 45-90 kg (100-200 lb) up to 300 m (980 ft).

Hauling rope

ASSAULT
Besiegers attack a fortress with scaling ladders while crossbowmen and handgunners cover the assault. The attackers are also using a cannon to blast holes in the stonework. More and more cannon were used in the 15th century to frighten defenders – some siege guns were enormous.

PULLING YOUR WEIGHT
The traction trebuchet worked in the same way as the counterpoise version, except that instead of a heavy weight the arm was moved by a team of men hauling on ropes. This meant that the machine was rather smaller than the counterpoise type and could not throw such large stones. But it could be reloaded more quickly. The sling was shorter and a man held it out as the arm began to rise – he had to remember to let go!

OLD AND NEW
A trebuchet towers over a gunner and his small cannon in this early 15th-century picture.

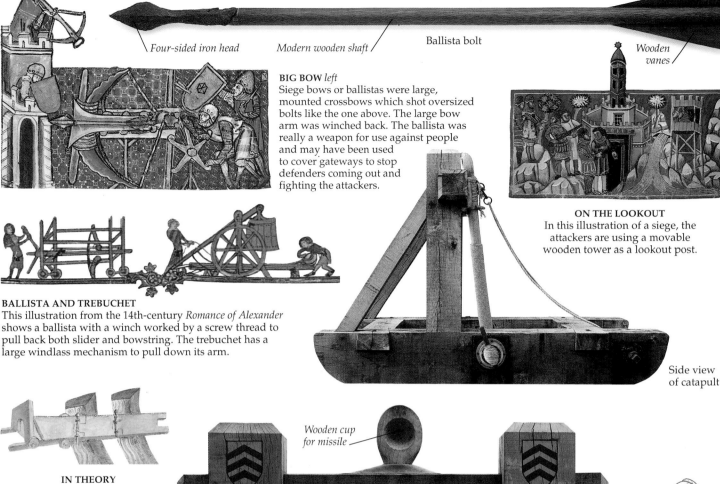

Four-sided iron head

Modern wooden shaft

Ballista bolt

Wooden vanes

BIG BOW *left*
Siege bows or ballistas were large, mounted crossbows which shot oversized bolts like the one above. The large bow arm was winched back. The ballista was really a weapon for use against people and may have been used to cover gateways to stop defenders coming out and fighting the attackers.

ON THE LOOKOUT
In this illustration of a siege, the attackers are using a movable wooden tower as a lookout post.

BALLISTA AND TREBUCHET
This illustration from the 14th-century *Romance of Alexander* shows a ballista with a winch worked by a screw thread to pull back both slider and bowstring. The trebuchet has a large windlass mechanism to pull down its arm.

Side view of catapult

IN THEORY
This is a design for a wooden bridge and covered penthouse to enable attackers to cross a ditch safely. It comes from a manuscript full of ingenious military ideas – many of which were probably not actually used.

Wooden cup for missile

Throwing arm

Rope to winch arm down

Skein of twisted ropes provides power

Catapult in use

SURRENDER
Formal surrender is made in this 15th-century illustration by handing the keys of the fortress to the besiegers. If taken after a siege a town or castle was sometimes looted by the soldiers because its occupants had refused to give up on request. On other occasions a truce would be made so that the person in charge of the castle could send to his lord for permission to surrender.

PULLING POWER
The catapult was used in the Roman Empire and was inherited by the soldiers of the Middle Ages. It used the pulling power of a skein of twisted ropes, sinews, or even hair, to force the arm up against a bar. When winched back and released, the arm flew up, releasing its missile from a wooden cup.

Front view of catapult

Arming for the fight

EARLY ARMOUR was quite easy to put on. Mail was pulled on over the head, while a coat of plates (pp. 12–13) was buckled at the back, or sides and shoulders. Plate armour was more complicated to put on but a knight could be armed by his squire in a few minutes and the armour could be speedily removed if necessary. After putting on a garment called an arming doublet, a knight was always armed from the feet upwards, finishing with the helmet. From the 15th century, some pieces of armour were laced to the arming doublet but in the following century these pieces were more usually attached to each other by straps or rivets. Here a squire is arming a knight in late 15th-century German "Gothic" style armour.

Mail gusset

Arming doublet

Waxed points

Cuisse

Poleyn

Greave

Sabaton

1 ARMING DOUBLET
This padded garment has waxed thongs (called points) to fasten different parts of the armour. Therefore the armour cannot be put on without the arming doublet. The mail gussets on the doublet cover the gaps which will be left by the plates.

2 SABATON, GREAVE, POLEYN, AND CUISSE
The sabaton and greave, for foot and lower leg, are followed by the poleyn which is attached to the cuisse. The top edge is laced up to the torso.

Backplate

Flanged edge

Breast-plate

Waist strap

3 MAIL SKIRT
Mail is secured around the waist to protect the groin, another area not fully covered by the plates. Using flexible mail here makes it easier to bend or sit.

4 BACKPLATE
The backplate is offered up into position. It has a flanged lower edge to deflect weapons from the buttocks and legs. A strap and buckle are riveted to the lower front edges.

5 BREASTPLATE
Breast and back together are called the cuirass. They are held together by the waist straps and are also connected at the shoulders.

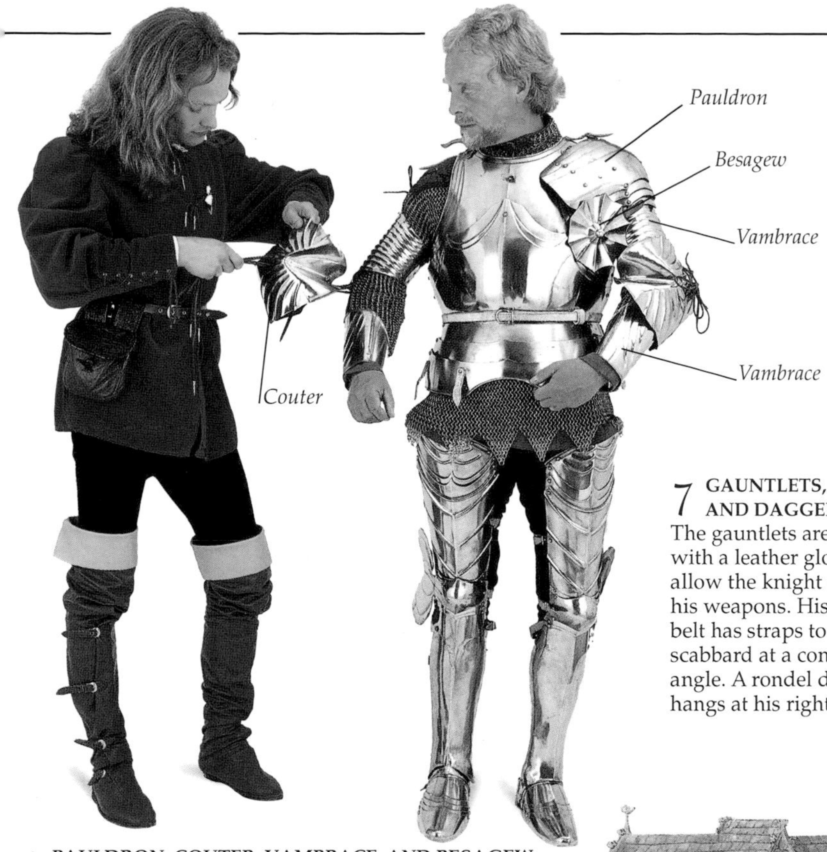

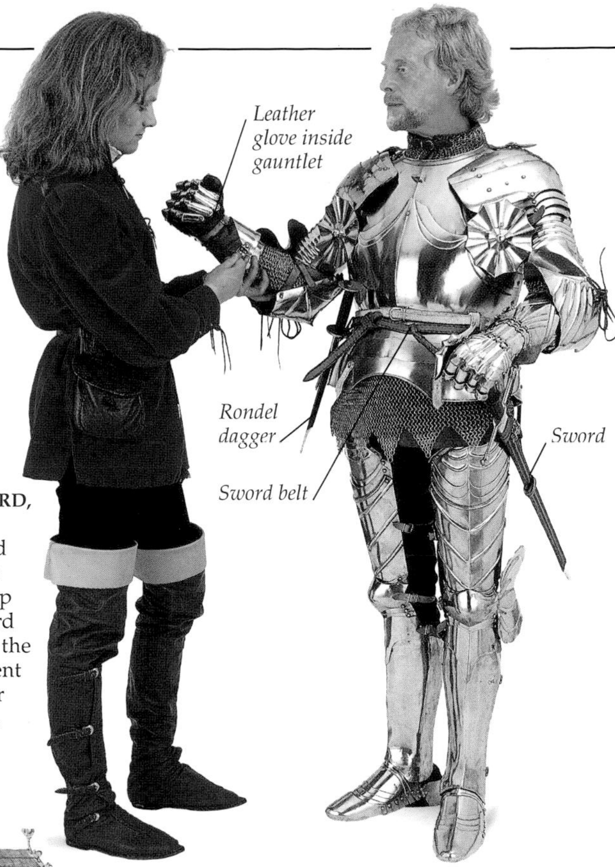

Pauldron

Besagew

Vambrace

Couter

Vambrace

7 GAUNTLETS, SWORD, AND DAGGER
The gauntlets are fitted with a leather glove to allow the knight to grip his weapons. His sword belt has straps to hold the scabbard at a convenient angle. A rondel dagger hangs at his right side.

Leather glove inside gauntlet

Rondel dagger

Sword belt

Sword

6 PAULDRON, COUTER, VAMBRACE, AND BESAGEW
The upper arm guard (vambrace) and elbow piece (couter) are tied by laces through pairs of holes in the plates. The pauldron and besagew guard the knight's shoulder and armpit.

ARMING A KNIGHT
A rare picture of about 1450 shows a knight being armed for foot combat in the lists. His arming doublet can be seen.

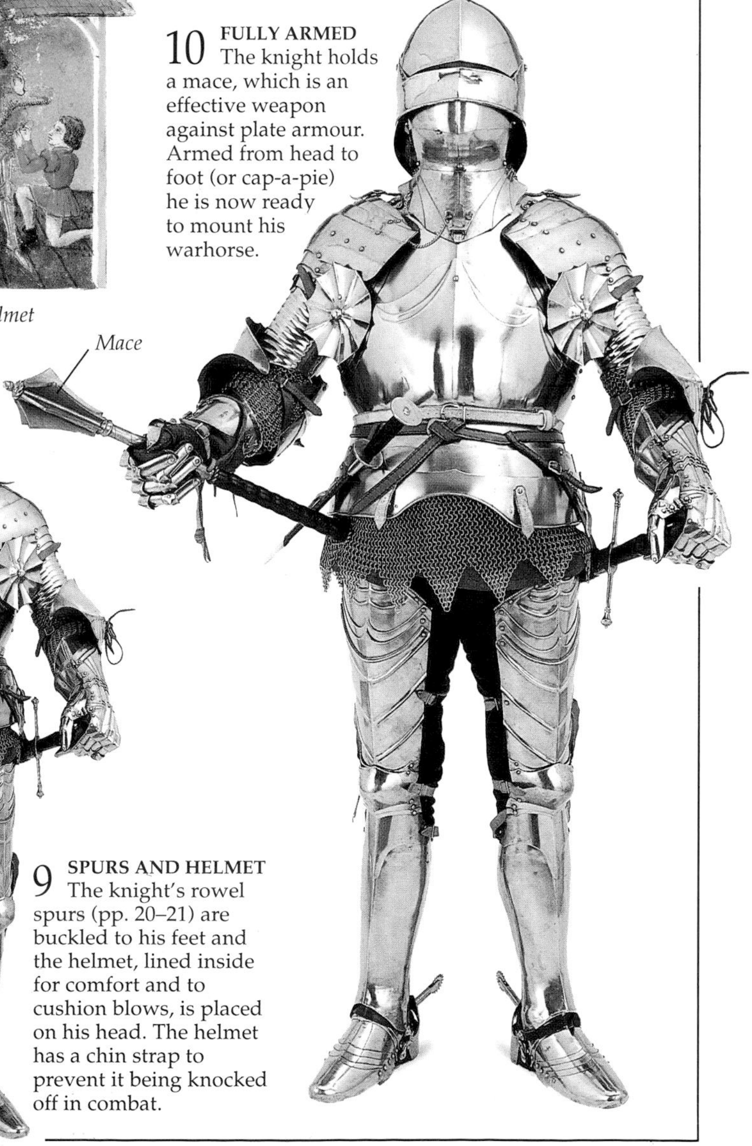

10 FULLY ARMED
The knight holds a mace, which is an effective weapon against plate armour. Armed from head to foot (or cap-a-pie) he is now ready to mount his warhorse.

Bevor

Helmet

Mace

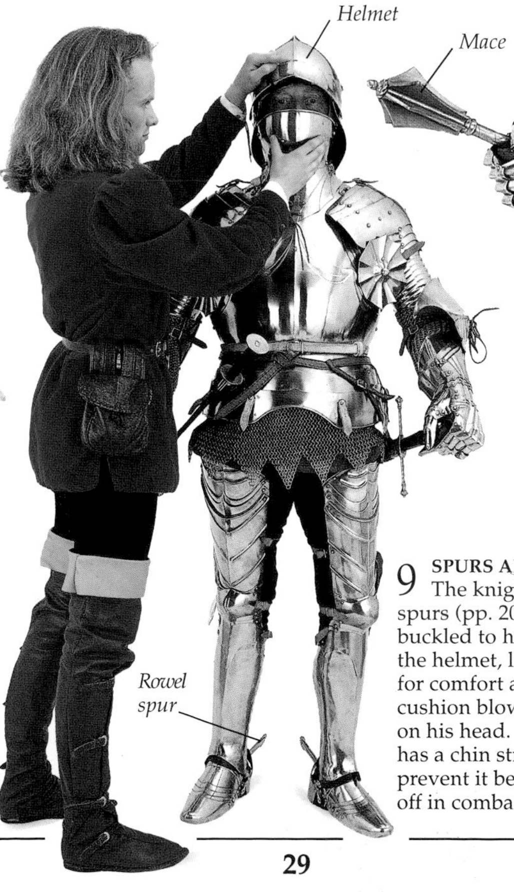

9 SPURS AND HELMET
The knight's rowel spurs (pp. 20–21) are buckled to his feet and the helmet, lined inside for comfort and to cushion blows, is placed on his head. The helmet has a chin strap to prevent it being knocked off in combat.

Rowel spur

8 BEVOR
A chin defence or bevor is added to protect the lower half of the face when wearing the sallet, a form of helmet especially popular in Germany.

The enemy

Knights soon found themselves facing infantry capable of defeating them. The English axemen at Hastings in 1066 cut down Norman knights, while Flemish footsoldiers with clubs defeated French horsemen at Courtrai in 1302. Massed Scottish spear formations stopped cavalry charges at Bannockburn in 1314, a strategy also favoured by the Swiss, using pikes. Different types of bow were highly effective against mounted knights. English longbowmen broke up cavalry charges by French knights at Crécy in 1346 and dismounted knights at Agincourt in 1415. The lethal crossbow shot short bolts from increasingly powerful weapons. In early 15th-century Bohemia (now part of the Czech lands) the Hussites blasted German knights, using the first massed guns, fired from the protection of wagons.

SLINGER
Some lightly armed infantrymen used slings. The stone or lead bullets were lethal if they struck a man in the face, and groups of slingers could force defenders to keep their heads down during sieges. However, they could not damage armour. Sometimes a sling was attached to a wooden handle to increase range – this was called a staff sling.

A BRISTLING HEDGE
Cavalrymen were unhappy about forcing their horses against spears, and infantry in close formation with a "hedge" of spears could hold off mounted knights. It then became necessary for archers to try and break up the formations by shooting missiles. The pike was even longer and more effective.

THE LONGBOW
This type of bow was usually made of a stave of yew wood about the height of the archer himself. It was usually fitted with horn nocks at the tips to take the hemp string. War bows probably needed a pull of at least 36 kg (80 lb) and many may have been far more powerful.

Barbed arrow-head

Leather bracer

Stave of yew wood

Horn nock to take string

Arrows stood in front for quick reloading

AN ARCHER
Longbows were used in many European countries, although on the mainland the crossbow was much more popular. The English used large numbers of archers, notably against the French during the Hundred Years War in the 14th and 15th centuries. In drawing a longbow the string was brought back somewhere between the cheek and the ear. The leather bracer protected the arms from an accidental slap from the string; a leather tab protected the drawer's fingers. Archers wore various pieces of defensive armour, or just a simple padded doublet, as here.

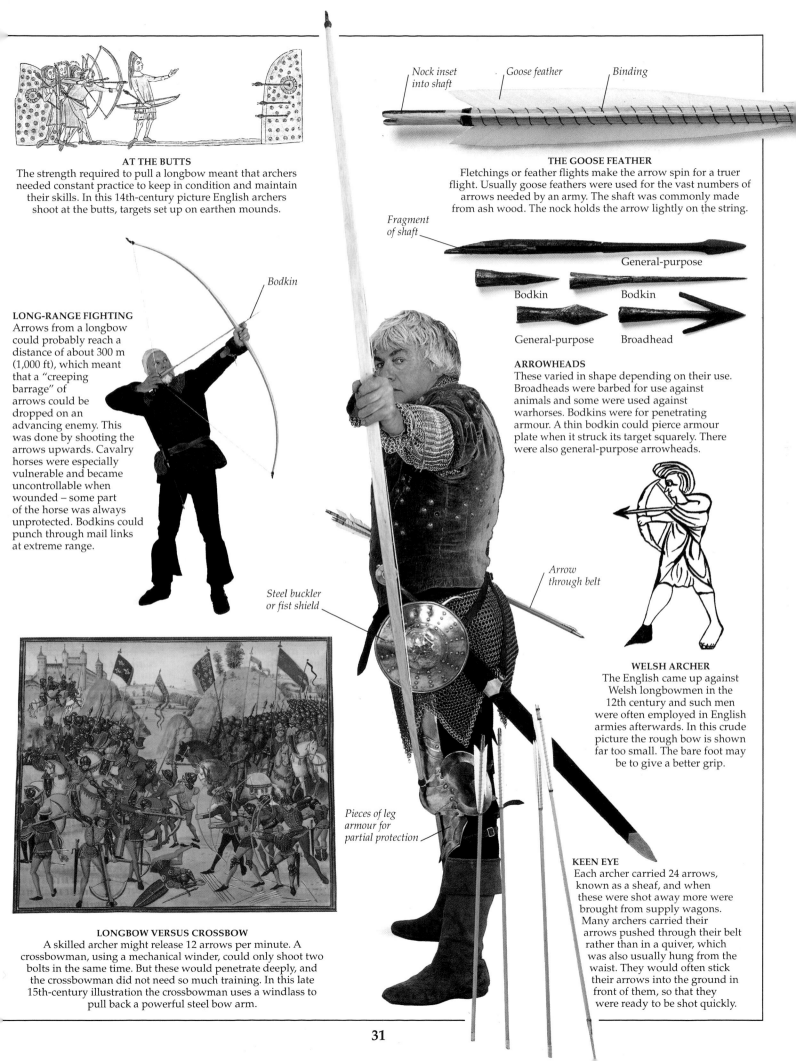

AT THE BUTTS
The strength required to pull a longbow meant that archers needed constant practice to keep in condition and maintain their skills. In this 14th-century picture English archers shoot at the butts, targets set up on earthen mounds.

Nock inset into shaft　　*Goose feather*　　*Binding*

THE GOOSE FEATHER
Fletchings or feather flights make the arrow spin for a truer flight. Usually goose feathers were used for the vast numbers of arrows needed by an army. The shaft was commonly made from ash wood. The nock holds the arrow lightly on the string.

Fragment of shaft

General-purpose

Bodkin　　Bodkin

General-purpose　　Broadhead

ARROWHEADS
These varied in shape depending on their use. Broadheads were barbed for use against animals and some were used against warhorses. Bodkins were for penetrating armour. A thin bodkin could pierce armour plate when it struck its target squarely. There were also general-purpose arrowheads.

LONG-RANGE FIGHTING
Arrows from a longbow could probably reach a distance of about 300 m (1,000 ft), which meant that a "creeping barrage" of arrows could be dropped on an advancing enemy. This was done by shooting the arrows upwards. Cavalry horses were especially vulnerable and became uncontrollable when wounded – some part of the horse was always unprotected. Bodkins could punch through mail links at extreme range.

Bodkin

Steel buckler or fist shield

Arrow through belt

WELSH ARCHER
The English came up against Welsh longbowmen in the 12th century and such men were often employed in English armies afterwards. In this crude picture the rough bow is shown far too small. The bare foot may be to give a better grip.

Pieces of leg armour for partial protection

LONGBOW VERSUS CROSSBOW
A skilled archer might release 12 arrows per minute. A crossbowman, using a mechanical winder, could only shoot two bolts in the same time. But these would penetrate deeply, and the crossbowman did not need so much training. In this late 15th-century illustration the crossbowman uses a windlass to pull back a powerful steel bow arm.

KEEN EYE
Each archer carried 24 arrows, known as a sheaf, and when these were shot away more were brought from supply wagons. Many archers carried their arrows pushed through their belt rather than in a quiver, which was also usually hung from the waist. They would often stick their arrows into the ground in front of them, so that they were ready to be shot quickly.

Into battle

THE RULES OF CHIVALRY dictated that knights should show courtesy
to defeated enemies. This was not just humane, it brought ransoms
from high-ranking prisoners. But this code was not always observed,
especially by desperate men facing death. For example, English
longbowmen supported by knights slaughtered French knights at
the battles of Crécy (1346), Poitiers (1356), and Agincourt (1415). And
knights often showed little mercy to foot soldiers, cutting them down
ruthlessly in pursuit. Much was at stake in a battle – defeat might
mean the loss of an army or even a throne. So commanders preferred
to ravage and raid enemy territory. This brought extra supplies as
well as destroying property and showed that the lord could not
protect his people in turn. Keeping troops close to an enemy's army
stopped it from
ravaging.

FIGHTING ON FOOT
Although knights were trained as
horsemen, they did not always
go into battle as cavalrymen. On
many occasions it was thought
better for a large part of an army
to dismount and form a solid
body, often supported by archers
and groups of cavalry. In this
late 14th-century illustration
dismounted English and French
knights and men-at-arms, many
wearing visored basinets on their
heads (pp. 12–13), clash on a
bridge. Archers and crossbowmen
assist them.

CALTROPS
These nasty-looking objects
are only a few centimetres
high. Made of iron, they
were scattered over the
ground before a battle to
lame horses or men from
the opposing army who
accidentally trod on them.
Whichever way they fell,
caltrops always landed with
one spike pointing upward.
They were also scattered in
front of castles.

IN PURSUIT *above*
A mid 13th-century battle scene shows the point
when one force in the battle has turned in
flight and is pursued by the other
side. Often the pursuers did not
hesitate to strike at men with their
backs turned, and once a man was down,
his opponent would give him several further cuts
to make sure he stayed there. Breaking ranks to
chase the enemy could sometimes put the rest of
your army in danger.

WALL OF HORSES *above*
Armour of the 12th century was similar in many parts of Europe, but fighting methods could vary. Instead of using their lances to stab overarm or even to throw, as sometimes happened in the 11th century, the Italian knights on this stone carving are "couching", or tucking, them under their arms. Each side charges in close formation, hoping to steamroller over their opponents.

One spike always points upward

SHOCK OF BATTLE
This late 15th-century picture shows the crash of two opposing cavalry forces in full plate armour and the deadly effects of well-aimed lances. Those struck down in the first line, even if only slightly wounded, were liable to be trampled by the horses either of the enemy or of their own knights following behind.

SPOILS OF WAR
When an army was defeated the victors would often capture the baggage. This could contain many valuables, especially if the leader was a prince. Captured towns also provided rich pickings and dead knights and prisoners were stripped of their armour after a battle. In this 14th-century Italian picture the victors are examining the spoils.

SHOCK WAVES
This early 16th-century German woodcut shows a disciplined charge by mounted knights. Spurring their horses to a gallop as they near the enemy, the first line has made contact while those behind follow with lances still raised. They will lower their lances before meeting their opponents.

Three spikes rest on the ground

33

The castle at peace

THE CASTLE DID NOT JUST house a garrison – it was home for the knight and his household. The most important building inside the castle was the great hall, where everyone had their meals, and day-to-day business was done. Sometimes there were also private rooms for the lord. There was also a kitchen (often outdoors in case of fire), a chapel, armourer's workshop, smithy, stables, kennels, pens for animals, and large storerooms to keep the castle well stocked. A water supply was vital, preferably a well, which could be used in times of siege. Outer walls might be whitewashed to protect against the weather; inner walls could be plastered and painted in attractive colours. Castles were useful resting places for nobles when they were travelling. When they were expected the domestic apartments were made ready and the floors might be covered with fresh straw, rushes, or sweet-smelling grasses.

SONG AND DANCE
Music was welcomed as entertainment and to accompany meals. Dances usually involved many people who often held hands in types of ring dance.

Coat-of-arms

WALL SCONCE
Only the rich could afford wax candles to burn in sconces like this 16th-century French example. Made of gilt copper, it bears the coat-of-arms of the Castelnau-LaLoubere family encircled by the collar of the Order of St. Michael.

SILVER CRUET
This silver vessel was kept in the chapel to hold the holy water or wine used in the Mass. It was made in Burgundy in the late 14th century.

AT THE LORD'S TABLE
At mealtimes the whole household would come together in the great hall. On this manuscript of about 1316, Lancelot entertains King Arthur by telling him about his adventures.

Limoges enamel decoration

SPIKED
This type of candlestick, called a pricket candlestick, had a long spike to take the candle. This one, dating to about 1230, was probably used in a castle chapel.

A GAME OF CHESS
King Francis I of France plays chess with Marguerite of Angouleme in a picture of about 1504. Being a wargame, chess was popular with knights. Chess pieces were often made of bone or ivory and beautifully carved.

BLAZING FIRE
Large fireplaces could be set in the thick stone walls of castles. The woman is spinning woollen thread (pp. 38–39).

Painted and tooled leather sheath

HAND BASIN
Pairs of basins like this, called gemellions, were used to wash peoples' hands at the table. A servant would pour water over the person's hands from one basin into the other and then dry the hands with a towel. Sometimes the water was poured from a ewer instead. This gemellion is decorated with Limoges enamels.

Household musician

A knight kneels before his lady

SERVING KNIVES
Pairs of broad-bladed knives like these 15th-century German ones were used for serving food. Each handle is mounted in brass and the grips have mahogany panels with plaques of stag horn. Each blade has an ancient swastika symbol. The leather sheath has lost its cap.

CHAMBER POT
Richer people might use chamber pots, like this one, for convenience, although castles often had lavatories built into the walls. These consisted of a seat connected to a shute which opened directly on to the outside of the castle wall.

PLAY THE GAME
Board games helped to pass long evenings. Here a young man of the early 14th century plays draughts or chequers with a lady. Backgammon was also popular.

Steelyard weight

BRONZE WEIGHTS
The late 13th-century steelyard weight was hung from a pivoting metal arm to work out the weight of an object placed on the other end. The weight on the right has the English royal arms in the version used after 1405.

Royal arms

The lord of the manor

SOME KNIGHTS were mercenary soldiers who fought simply for money. Others, particularly until the 13th century, lived at their lord's expense as household troops in his castle. But others were given pieces of land by their lord. Such a man became lord of the manor and lived off its produce. He lived in a manor house, often of stone and with its own defences. He held a large part of the manor as the home farm and "his" peasants, workers of varying status, owed him service in return for their homes. They had to bake their bread in his oven and pay for the privilege. The lord received part of their goods, as did the church, although they might be invited to feasts at festivals such as Lammas (when bread made from the season's first corn was blessed). The lord sat in judgment in the manor court and might have a house in a town for business dealings.

HOME DEFENCE
Stokesay is a fortified manor house in Shropshire, England. It consists of a hall and chamber block with a tower at each end, mostly built in the late 13th century. In the 17th century a half-timbered gallery was added.

Original die

MY SEAL ON IT
Noblemen often could not read or write. Instead of signing a document they added a wax seal, pressed from a metal die. This is the silver seal die, with a modern cast, of Robert FitzWalter, one of the leaders of the rebel English barons who made King John sign Magna Carta in 1215.

ALL IN THE GAME
This wealthy 14th-century Italian couple while away the time with a board game. Otherwise entertainment for the knight was limited to resident or strolling players, musicians, or poets.

Modern cast

Name of Robert FitzWalter, owner of the seal

IVORY CHESS PIECES
These Scandinavian chessmen, found on the Isle of Lewis, Scotland, are carved from walrus ivory and date from the mid 12th century.

Queen

King

Bishop

Knight

Warder (Rook)

UPHILL STRUGGLE

The medieval peasant had a life of hard work in the fields, growing and harvesting the crops. The 14th-century Luttrell Psalter shows peasants trying to coax a hay cart up a steep slope.

THE LORD

The status and rank of a lord varied, as did the size of his manor. Some lords were powerful men who held a number of manors, visiting them as necessary. A bailiff would look after the running of the estates when the lord was away. He might go on trips to a town where merchants carried on their trade and where lords in need of money could borrow it from money-lenders.

GARDEN OF DELIGHT

One of the houses on this 15th-century manor is made of a framework of timbers filled in with wattle and daub (mud or clay), which has been whitewashed. Close by is an orchard of fruit trees.

LIKE FATHER, LIKE SON

These details from an altar frontal of about 1500 show a knight in prayer, with his seven sons. Large families were common. The eldest son would follow his father and become a knight (pp. 10–11). Daughters would hope to marry noblemen (pp. 38–39). Younger sons and daughters often went into the church.

DECORATED CASKET

This large casket belonged to a rich family of the early 15th century. It is made of wood covered in bone panels carved with biblical scenes from the story of Susanna and the Elders.

The lady of the manor

THE LIFE OF THE LADY
The lady ruled the domestic areas – the kitchens and living quarters – of the castle or manor house. She had officials to run the household affairs, but she had to check the accounts and agree to any expenses. It was her duty to receive guests courteously and arrange for their accommodation. Ladies-in-waiting were her companions, maidservants attended her, and nurses looked after her children. The children were very important, for the lady's main role in medieval society was to provide heirs.

In THE MIDDLE AGES women, even those of noble rank, had far fewer rights than a woman can expect today. Young women were often married by the age of 14. A girl's family would arrange her marriage and she would be given a dower, a gift to pass on to her husband. On marriage a woman's inheritance passed to the husband, so knights were often on the lookout for a rich heiress to marry. But the lady was her husband's equal in private life. She could provide great support for her husband and take responsibility for the castle when he was away. She might even have to defend the castle if it was besieged and hold it against her enemies.

DALLIANCE
The ideal of courtly love is shown in an illustration from the medieval poem *The Romance of the Rose*. Women pass the time pleasantly, listening to a song while a fountain pours water into an ornamental stream. In reality, many women would not have had time for such activities.

THE WHITE SWAN
This gold and enamelled brooch is known as the Dunstable Swan and dates from the early 15th century. The swan was used as a badge by the House of Lancaster (one of the English ruling families), particularly by the Princes of Wales. Noblewomen might wear such badges to show their allegiance.

WOMEN OF ACCOMPLISHMENT
Ladies were often very well educated. Some could read and write, understand Latin, and speak foreign languages. In this picture of the 1460s, learned ladies with books represent Philosophy and the Liberal Arts.

ON BENDED KNEES
A knight of about 1200 places his hands in those of his lady in an act of homage like that performed by a subordinate to his lord. In this case he is indicating that he will be his lady's servant – an ideal of courtly love that was not borne out in practice.

BAD NEWS
A lady swoons on receiving news of her husband's death. Although marriages were arranged by the couples' families, husband and wife could and did become extremely fond of one another and sometimes grew to love each other.

"SUITABLE" OCCUPATIONS
Women were expected to know how to spin wool, but some men thought teaching them to read was dangerous! In this early 15th-century picture one woman spins woollen thread while another cards or combs out the wool.

Flemish gold brooch

JEWELS
Women liked to display their rank by wearing rings and brooches. The 15th-century gold brooch at the top is probably Flemish and has a female figure among the precious stones. The late 14th-century English brooch is decorated with coiled monsters.

English gold brooch

Pommel

Cantle

TALE ON A SADDLE
This German saddle dates from between about 1440 and 1480. It is made of wood covered with plaques of staghorn, on which are carved the figure of a man and a woman repeated several times. Inlaid hard wax provides the colour. The figures' speech is written on scrolls. They speak of their love and the woman asks: "But if the war should end?"

SIDESADDLE
Noblewomen were often active hunters. This medallion of 1477 shows Mary of Burgundy. She carries her hawk on her wrist and is riding sidesaddle, a method that solved the difficulty of sitting on a horse in a long dress. Her mount wears a decorative cloth trapper.

Carved plaque

The ideal of chivalry

ALTHOUGH KNIGHTS were men of war, they traditionally behaved in a courteous and civil way when dealing with their enemies. In the 12th century this kind of behaviour was extended to form a knightly code of conduct, with a special emphasis on courtly manners towards women. The poems of courtly love recited by the troubadours of southern France were based on this code, and the romance stories which became popular in the 13th century showed the ways a warrior should behave.

Churchmen liked the idea of high standards and made the knighting ceremony a religious occasion with a church vigil and purifying bath (pp. 10–11). Books on chivalry also appeared, though in reality knights often found it difficult to live up to the ideal.

GEORGE AND THE DRAGON
St. George was a soldier martyred by the Romans in about A.D. 350. During the Middle Ages stories appeared telling how he rescued a king's daughter from a dragon. He became especially connected with England. This carved ivory shows St. George with the battlements of a castle in the background.

KNIGHT IN SHINING ARMOUR
This 15th-century tournament parade shield depicts a bareheaded knight kneeling before his lady. The words on the scroll mean "You or death", and the figure of death is represented by a skeleton.

TRUE-LOVE KNOTS
Medallions like this were sometimes made to mark special occasions, such as marriages. This one was struck to commemorate the marriage of Margaret of Austria to the Duke of Savoy in 1502. The knots in the background are the badge of Savoy – they also refer to the way the couple's love will unite the two families.

WHAT'S IN A NAME?
This scene, from the 15th-century book *The Lovelorn Heart*, by Frenchman René of Anjou, illustrates the strange world of the medieval romance in which people can stand for objects or feelings. Here the knight, called Cueur (meaning Heart), reads an inscription while his companion, Desire, lies sleeping.

LANCELOT AND GUINEVERE
King Arthur was probably a fifth-century warrior, but the legends of the king and the knights of the round table gained popularity in 13th-century Europe. They tell of Arthur's struggles against evil and the love between Arthur's queen, Guinevere, and Sir Lancelot, which eventually led to the destruction of his court. In this story, Lancelot crosses a sword bridge to rescue Guinevere.

THE KNIGHT OF THE CART
Knights rode on horseback and it was usually thought a disgrace for a knight to travel in a cart. This picture shows an episode from the story of Sir Lancelot. Lancelot was famous for his valour and skill in combat, but his love affair with Queen Guinevere brought him shame. In this episode Lancelot meets a dwarf who offers to tell him where Guinevere is if he will ride in the cart.

ROYAL CHAMPION
Sir Edward Dymoke was the champion of Queen Elizabeth I. At her coronation banquet in Westminster, it was his job to ride fully armed into the hall and hurl his gauntlet to the ground to defy anyone who wished to question the queen's right to rule. Such a challenge was made at every English coronation until that of George IV in 1821.

Lock

Corner reinforcement

TRAGIC LOVERS
The ivory carvings on this 12th-century box show episodes from the story of Tristan and Iseult. This is a tale of the knight Tristan, who accidentally drank a love potion and fell in love with Iseult, the bride of his uncle, King Mark.

The tournament

Fighting men have always trained for battle, and tournaments started, probably in the 11th century, as practice for war. Two teams of knights fought a mock battle, called a tourney or mêlée, over a huge area of countryside, sometimes even assisted by footsoldiers. Defeated knights gave up their horse and armour to the victor, so a good fighter could make a fortune. At first, battle armour and sharp weapons were used, but blunted weapons were introduced in the 13th century. Other contests, such as jousts (pp. 44–45) and combat on foot (pp. 46–47), also appeared. In the *pas d'armes*, popular in the 15th century, one or more contestants held the tournament ground, or lists, and sent challenges to other knights and squires. In the 17th century the tournament was replaced in most countries by displays of horsemanship called carousels.

"Roped" comb

BIRD MEN ON PARADE
In the early 16th century it became fashionable to wear helmets with strange, mask-like visors in the parades during tournaments. Sometimes knights even wore them during the tourney itself. The visors were fitted to otherwise normal close-helmets (pp. 14–15). This one is like an eagle's head, with feathers etched into the metal.

Eagle's beak

Breaths for ventilation

WITH BANNERS FLYING
The colourful array of banners at a tournament was ideal for the display of coats-of-arms and all kinds of other fanciful designs. The knights also wore large crests on their helms even when these were no longer worn in battle.

Devil

DEVIL TAKE YOU
Although tournaments were popular with knights, and many people liked to watch, the church frowned on them because so much blood was often spilt. In this early 14th-century picture, devils wait to seize the souls of knights killed in a tourney.

A KNIGHT DISGRACED
The women viewed the banners and crested helms of the contestants before the tourney. If a lady knew that one of the knights had done wrong, his helm was taken down and he was banned from the lists. This picture comes from the 15th-century tournament book of René of Anjou.

CLUB TOURNEY

In this type of tourney two teams using blunt swords and clubs will try to knock the crests off their opponents' helmets which are fitted with protective face grilles. Each knight has a banner-bearer, while attendants (called varlets) stand ready in case he falls. The knight of honour rides between two ropes which separate the teams; ladies and judges are in the stands. Although the lists had become smaller the artist of this picture has squashed them up to fit everything in.

Hole to take lance

Etched and gilt decoration

Vamplate

Plume holder

Face embossed in metal

VAMPLATE AND LOCKING-GAUNTLET

The circular vamplate was fixed over the lance to guard the knight's hand. Once the knight had gripped his sword the locking-gauntlet was locked shut so the sword was not lost in combat. It found favour in the 16th century. Both objects are from an Italian armour of about 1570.

PARADE CASQUE

This Italian open helmet of about 1530 was worn in parades. It has embossed decoration and the face has been given a plate shaped like teeth. It may once have had a lower set of teeth as well. The hinged ear pieces are missing.

Metal plate imitating teeth

Neck guard

Locking-gauntlet

The joust

DURING THE 13TH CENTURY a dramatic new element was added to the tournament – jousts, in which knights fought one-to-one. In a joust, a knight could show his skill without other contestants getting in the way. Usually the knights fought on horseback with lances, though in some contests they continued the fight with swords. Two knights would charge towards one another at top speed and try to unhorse each other with a single blow of the lance. You could also score points if you broke your lance on your opponent's shield. Sometimes they used sharp lances in combats called "jousts of war". These could kill a knight, so many jousters preferred to use a lance fitted with a blunt tip or with a coronel shaped like a small crown to spread the impact. Such combats were called "jousts of peace". Special armour was developed for jousting, to increase protection. A barrier called the tilt was introduced in the 15th century to separate the knights and avoid collisions.

Eye slit

FROG-MOUTHED HELM
This 15th-century helmet for the jousts of peace was originally fastened down the back and front. The wearer could see his opponent by leaning forward during the charge. At the moment of impact he straightened up, so that the "frog-mouthed" lower lip protected his eyes from the lance-head or fragments of the shaft.

Curved edge to support lance

GERMANIC JOUSTERS
In the Germanic countries, knights often practised the "Rennen", a version of the jousts of war. As no barrier was used, the knights' legs were partially protected by metal shields. The shields above their heads show that in this version they could be struck off.

LANCER'S SHIELD
This late 15th-century wooden shield is covered in leather. It was probably used for the Rennen. The lance could be placed in the recess in the side. The shield was attached to the breastplate by means of a staple nailed to the rear.

BREAKING A LANCE
Lances were made of wood and by the 16th century were often fluted to help them splinter easily. This 17th-century lance is slightly thinner than those used for jousting against an opponent. It was used to spear a small ring hanging from a bracket.

PARADE BEFORE THE TILT
Knights paraded beside the tilt, or barrier, before the jousting commenced. This scene from Froissart's *Chronicles* was painted in the late 15th century, although it depicts the jousts at St. Inglevert which took place in 1390, before the tilt was introduced. Attendants with spare lances accompany the knights.

Reinforcing bevor

Grandguard reinforced the wearer's left shoulder

Bolt joining grandguard to the reinforcing breastplate and to the breastplate behind

Protruding arm to support lance

LANCE-REST
This was fixed to the breastplate by staples. It helped to take the weight of the lance and stopped it from sliding back through the armpit on impact.

Large reinforcing gauntlet, here with flexible mitten-style finger plates

REINFORCEMENTS
Knights took part in many different types of combat, so armours were sometimes supplied with additional pieces to allow them to be made up in various ways. The reinforcing pieces shown here are from South Germany and date to about 1550. They are for a version of the jousts of peace known as the "tilt in the Italian fashion". Extra protection is provided mainly for the left side of the body, because the knights passed one another on that side. Knights did not need great manoeuvrability when jousting, so rigid extra pieces could be bolted on. These were often heavier or thicker pieces than those used on field armour. This meant that the armour was heavy and difficult to move around in, but this did not matter, because such armour did not have to be worn for long periods and safety was a priority.

Pasguard bolted to the front of the couter or elbow defence

Strap secures a reinforcing tasset to the wearer's left side, where the greatest protection is needed

Reinforcing tasset

OLD-STYLE JOUSTING
These 15th-century knights are jousting in the old style, without a barrier. This style remained especially popular in the German countries. The knights' lances are fitted with coronels and are placed in the shield recesses.

WATERY WARRIORS
A version of the joust was sometimes carried out on water, as this early 14th-century miniature shows. Two teams of rowers propelled their boats towards one another whilst a man in the prow of each tried to knock his opponent off balance.

Foot combat

IN SOME 13TH-CENTURY JOUSTS the knights dismounted after using their lances and continued fighting with swords. By the 14th century, such foot combats were popular in their own right. Each contestant was allowed a set number of blows, delivered alternately, and men-at-arms stood ready to separate them if they got too excited. From 15th-century writings we learn that each man sometimes threw a javelin first, then the fight went on with sword, axe, or staff weapon. Later still, such combats were replaced by contests in which two teams fought across a barrier. It was called the foot tournament because, as in the mounted tourney (pp. 42–43), each man tried to break a spear against his opponent before continuing the fight with blunted swords.

AT THE READY
This detail from a 16th-century Flemish tapestry shows contestants waiting to take part in foot combat over the barrier. A page is handing one knight his helmet.

Sword cuts

Visor

Holes for laces of cross-straps to hold the head inside

Chin piece

FORMAL FIGHT
Foot combats in the 15th century took place without a barrier, so the contestants protected their legs with armour. The most common helmet for these contests was the great basinet (pp. 12–13), which was outdated for war by the middle of the century.

Hand-threaded screw

BROW REINFORCE
This plate was screwed to the visor of the close-helmet shown on the right. It gave more protection to the left side of the head.

CLOSE-HELMET
This helmet was designed for the tournament on foot. It is so richly gilded that it is surprising that it was ever worn in actual combat. But the sword cuts show that it must have been used. It was part of a dazzling garniture of gilt armour made in 1555.

Hole for hearing

Visor

Bevor

Eye slit

EXCHANGE VISOR
Two threaded bolts allowed the visor to be removed from the helmet on the left and replaced with this one, which has a number of ventilation holes. It could be used for battle or for foot combat.

Lifting peg

Pivoting fork for holding up bevor

ARMET
In this type of helmet the cheek-pieces pivot outwards when it is put on, instead of the front half of the helmet swinging up as in the helmet at top right. This German example of about 1535 has a visor that fits inside the rim of the bevor, where it is held by a spring-catch. The bevor is locked over the cheek-piece in the same way.

TRIAL BY BATTLE
Not all foot contests were held for sport. Sometimes a charge of murder or treason was settled by a combat, in which God was thought to help the innocent man. The contest went on until one was either killed or surrendered, in which case he was executed.

POLLAXE
This weapon was very popular in battle and foot combat. It was used to strike the opponent's head (the word poll means head) and the solid hammer-head at the back could concuss a man in armour. The long langets of this example of about 1470 helped to hold the head firmly and prevent the shaft being cut when fighting.

FOOT-COMBAT ARMOUR
This German armour of about 1580 forms part of a garniture, or collection of pieces. Some larger garnitures could be made into several different armours. The surface was originally blued, and is etched and gilded, with the ornament outlined in black. The visor and upper bevor lock together with a bolt. This stops them from accidentally flying open if struck, a safety feature of some foot-combat helmets. No leg armour was worn because the combat took place over a barrier and blows below this level were forbidden.

Plate to deflect side blows from the head

Pauldron

Langet

Rondel protects the hand

Gauntlet

THE BARRIER
This crude drawing of the late 16th-century shows knights taking part in a foot contest over the barrier.

Heraldry

Or, a pale gules

Azure, a fess embattled or

Sable, a cross engrailed or

Lozengy argent and gules

Vert, a crescent or

Azure, a fleur-de-lys or

Gules, a spur argent

M EN HAD ALWAYS decorated their shields. In the 12th century these designs became more standardized in a system known as heraldry, enabling a knight to be identified by symbols on his shield, or a full coat-of-arms. It is often said that this was done because helmets with faceguards made knights difficult to recognize, but a more likely reason was the need to identify contestants in tournaments. Heraldry was based on strict rules. Only one coat-of-arms was carried by a knight, and this passed to his eldest son when he died. Other children used variants of their father's arms. Arms used a series of standard colours and "metals" (silver or gold) and are described in a special language, based on Old French.

BADGE OF OFFICE
This copper arm badge was worn by a servant of François de Lorraine, Hospitaller Prior of France from 1549 to 1563, whose arms it bears. Retainers of a lord often wore his livery badge.

COSTUME DESIGN
The fleur-de-lys, heraldic emblem of France, is used to decorate this long tunic, although true heraldry forbids gold placed on white or silver. The fur lining of the mantle was also adapted for heraldic purposes.

ROLL OF ARMS
Heralds made lists to keep a record of participants in military events like tournaments and battles. The Carlisle Roll contains 277 shields of King Edward III's retinue on his visit to Carlisle, England, in 1334.

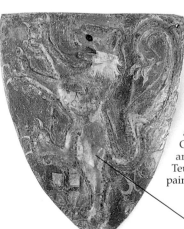

A KNIGHT'S SHIELD
This rare surviving shield of the 13th century is made from wood, which has a lion rampant moulded in leather. These are the arms of a landgrave (ruler) of Hesse in Germany. He is represented as a knight of the Teutonic Order, as the white shield and black cross of the Teutonic knights has been painted on the lower left.

Lion rampant

HERALDIC JAR
Coats-of-arms were placed on all sorts of objects, to show ownership or simply to add colour. This jar of about 1500 has quartered arms, in which the arms of two families joined by marriage appear twice together.

Arms of Cosimo de' Medici

COLOURFUL SPECTACLE
In this 15th-century picture, shields of the knightly passengers are hung over the sides of boats, largely for display. Colourful heraldic banners bore the arms of their knightly owners and were a rallying point in battle, as were the longer standards, which carried a lord's badges and other devices. Here the French royal arms appear on trumpet banners.

MAKING AN IMPRESSION
The bezel of this large gold 14th-century signet ring is engraved with heraldic arms which include those of the de Grailly family. Above are the letters: "EID Gre", probably meaning: "This is the seal of Jean de Grailly". When pressed into hot wax used to seal a document the arms appeared in the wax the right way around.

SWORD ARMS
This Italian falchion or short cutting sword dates from the mid 16th century. It is etched with the arms of Cosimo de' Medici, Duke of Florence. It is encircled with the collar of the Order of the Golden Fleece, one of several knightly orders of chivalry.

Pommel of gilt bronze cast in shape of a lion's head

COAT-OF-ARMS
The brass of Sir Thomas Blenerhasset (died 1531) shows the heraldic arms on his coat armour, the name given to the surcoat. The version worn by this date is the tabard, also used by heralds.

SPANISH PLATE
The Spanish kingdom of Castile had a castle for its arms, while that of Leon used a lion. These are the earliest quartered arms, first noted in 1272. On this Spanish dish of about 1425 the true heraldic colours have been ignored, while the background has designs influenced by the Spanish Muslims.

Gules a lion rampant or

Or, a lion sejant regardant purpure

Gules, a swan argent

Azure, a dolphin naiant argent

Or, a dragon rampant vert

Or, a portcullis purpure

Azure, a sun in splendour or

KEY TO LABELS ON ARMS	
Or	Gold
Argent	Silver
Gules	Red
Azure	Blue
Sable	Black
Vert	Green
Purpure	Purple

Hunting and hawking

MEDIEVAL MONARCHS AND LORDS were passionately fond of hunting and hawking. The sport provided fresh meat, as well as helping to train knights for war and allowing them to show their courage when facing dangerous animals like the wild boar. The Norman kings set aside vast areas of woodland for hunting in England, and there were severe penalties for poachers or anyone who broke the forest laws. The animals hunted ranged from deer and boar to birds and rabbits. Knights often hunted on horseback, which provided excitement and useful practice for war. Sometimes beaters drove the prey towards the huntsmen, who lay in wait. Hunters might also use bows or crossbows, which gave them good experience with these weapons. Hawking was very popular, and good birds were prized. One 15th-century manuscript gives a list of hawks, showing how only the higher members of society could fly the best birds.

FLYING TO A LURE
A lure was a dummy bird which the falconer swung from a long cord. The falcon would pounce on the lure, so that the falconer could retrieve his bird. The lure could also be used to exercise a bird or teach it to climb high and "stoop" down on its prey.

NOBLE BEASTS
This detail of the carving on the side of the crossbow tiller shows a stag hunt. Only rich people were allowed to hunt stags.

Steel pin to engage rack for spanning bow

Wooden tiller veneered with polished stag horn carved in relief

Wooden flights

WOODEN FEATHERS
These German crossbow bolts date to about 1470. One has wooden flights rather than the feathers usually seen on arrows.

FOR DEER HUNTERS *below*
The blade of a German hunting sword of about 1540 is etched with scenes of a stag hunt. Such swords were carried when hunting and also for general protection.

WOLF HUNT
When hunting for wolves, huntsmen would hang pieces of meat in a thicket and drag them along pathways to leave a scent. Look-outs in trees warned of the wolf's approach and mastiff dogs flushed it out for the hunters. This hunt is pictured in a copy of the late 14th-century hunting book of Gaston Phoebus, Count of Foix, France.

FREDERICK II THE FALCONER
This German emperor was so keen on falconry that in the mid 13th century he wrote a book on the subject, from which this picture comes. Some lords even kept hawks in their private apartments.

Deer being driven into nets

Dogs chasing the deer

Hunting horn

Man shooting squirrel

Falconer

ON THE HUNT
A Flemish or German silver plaque of about 1600 shows hunting with hounds, falconry, and shooting. One hound catches a hare in front of three ladies who watch with interest from their carriage.

WEAPON AT THE READY
The crossbow was a popular hunting weapon. It could be used on horseback and easily reloaded using a goat's-foot lever or a ratchet and winder mechanism called a rack. Because the bowstring was drawn back over the nut and held there until released by the trigger, the crossbow could be spanned ready in case any game was flushed out. Crossbows for use in hunting were sometimes lavishly decorated. On this example of 1450–1470 the coat-of-arms of the owner is painted on the tiller and there are carved panels showing hunting scenes.

Original bow-string of twisted cord

Revolving nut released by trigger below

Triunglar barbed head

PET CARE
Hunting dogs needed careful looking after and Gaston Phoebus recommends the use of herbal medicines to cure mange, diseases of the eye, ear and throat, and even rabies. Swollen paws damaged by thorns or gorse required attention. Dislocated shoulders were treated by bonesetters and broken legs put in harnesses.

BOAR-CATCHER
The boar spear was a stout weapon intended to stop an onrushing boar or even a bear. To stop the blade going too far into the animal, a cross-bar was provided. Boar sword blades were also pierced for a cross-bar.

The tusks of the aggressive boar were highly dangerous

AFTER THEM!
Ladies could also be avid hunters. In this illustration of about 1340 a lady blows a hunting horn as she gallops after the dogs.

Faith and pilgrimage

THE CHURCH PLAYED A MAJOR PART in the life of the Middle Ages. Western Europe was Roman Catholic until Protestantism took hold in some countries in the 16th century. Most people held strong beliefs and churches flourished, taking one-tenth of everyone's goods as a sort of tax called a tithe. Monasteries were sometimes founded by wealthy lords, partly to make up for their sins. Some lords actually became monks after a life of violence, hoping that this would make it easier for them to enter heaven. To get help from dead saints, Christians would make pilgrimages to well-known shrines, such as the tomb of St. Peter in Rome, and wear a symbolic badge. Holy relics, many of them forgeries, were carried for protection.

OWNER OF THE HORN
This medallion shows Charles Duke of Burgundy who owned the Horn of St. Hubert in the late 15th century.

Container for Holy Water

WATER CARRIER
People wore tiny containers called ampullae holding Holy Water to protect themselves from evil. This one has a picture of St. Thomas Becket, killed at Canterbury in 1170, and would have been bought after a pilgrimage to his shrine.

Lead pilgrim badge of St. Catherine martyred on a wheel

KNIGHT AT PRAYER
The saints played a vital part in peoples' lives. This stained-glass window from the Netherlands shows a knight from the Bernericourt family praying at a statue of Mary Magdelene.

SILVER CHALICE
A chalice was used to hold the consecrated wine during the Mass. This one, which was made in Spain or Italy in the early 16th century, is richly decorated, showing the wealth and importance of the church. It is decorated with six medallions which show Christ and some of the Saints, including St. James of Compostella. Pilgrims to his tomb wore badges bearing his emblem of a scallop shell.

Head of saint

Lead seal showing the Virgin Mary holding baby Jesus

SYMBOLS OF FAITH
People often wore badges to show that they had been on a pilgrimage. The simple lead cross shows the importance of this sign – even a knight's sword guard could be used as one. Other popular subjects were Christ and the Virgin Mary and the saints.

HORN OF ST. HUBERT
Medieval people liked to touch or even possess relics of the dead saints, even though some had no connection with the real saint. St. Hubert was said to have seen the vision of a cross shining between a deer's antlers, and he became the patron saint of huntsmen.

Pelican in her piety

St. John

Virgin Mary

Crucified Christ

TO BE A PILGRIM
These 15th-century pilgrims are travelling to the Holy Land. Jerusalem, where Christ had been crucified and buried, was the greatest goal, but getting there meant a long and dangerous journey. Pilgrims to Jerusalem were called "palmers" and wore a palm-leaf badge.

MISSIONARY
The Church was always keen to convert others to Christianity, either through peaceful teaching or by more forceful methods like those used by the Teutonic knights in Eastern Europe. Here Friar Oderic receives a blessing before he goes to the East as a missionary. Knights might also desire a blessing before undertaking dangerous tasks or journeys.

St. Nicholas

THE CANTERBURY TALES
Geoffrey Chaucer (right) wrote *The Canterbury Tales* in about 1386. These concern a group of pilgrims who travel from London to the Shrine of Thomas Becket in Canterbury. A knight (left) and his son, a squire, join the group, who tell stories along the way to pass the time.

Chaucer's knight

Geoffrey Chaucer

PROCESSIONAL CROSS
This early 15th-century Italian silver cross has been partly gilded and decorated with enamels. The Virgin Mary, St. John and St. Nicholas are shown on the arms of the cross. The pelican is a symbol of piety – people thought that she wounded herself in order to feed her young, symbol of Christ bleeding for all sinners.

The crusades

In 1095 at Clermont, France, Pope Urban II launched a military expedition to take the Christian Holy Places in Jerusalem back from the Seljuk Turks who ruled the Holy Land. This expedition became known as the First Crusade. A huge army travelled thousands of kilometres across Europe, gathering at Constantinople (now Istanbul) before going on to capture Jerusalem in 1099. But the city was soon retaken by the Muslims and many other crusades failed to take it back, apart from a brief period in 1228-29 when the German emperor, Frederick II, made an agreement with the Muslims. Even Richard Lionheart, the warlike English king and a leader of the Third Crusade of 1190, knew that if he could capture the city, he would not be able to hold it. Nevertheless, western leaders set up feudal states in the Holy Land. The fall of Acre in 1291 marked the end of one of these states, though Christians still fought Muslims in Spain and the Mediterranean, and Slavs in Eastern Europe. Crusades were also preached against non-Catholic heretics in Europe.

PEOPLE'S CRUSADE
In 1096 the French preacher Peter the Hermit led an undisciplined mob from Cologne in Germany towards Jerusalem. On their way they pillaged and looted, killing Jews for their money and because they thought them responsible for Christ's death. Though there were some knights in this People's Crusade, it was wiped out in Anatolia (modern Turkey) by the Turks.

SPANISH CRUSADERS
Muslims, known as Moors, had lived in Spain since the eighth century. From the 11th century Christian armies tried to push them back south until Granada, their last stronghold, fell to the Christians in 1492. Warrior monks, such as the Order of Santiago, seen in this 13th-century picture, helped the Christian reconquest of Spain.

TAKING SHIP
There were two routes from Europe to the Holy Land: the dangerous road overland or across the Mediterranean Sea. The Italian city states of Venice, Pisa, and Genoa, eager for new trade, often provided ships. Unfortunately in 1204 Venice persuaded the leaders of the fourth Crusade to attack the Byzantine capital of Constantinople, which never recovered.

THE MAMLUKS
An elite body of troops, the Mamluks were recruited from slaves by the Muslims. This late 13th- or early 14th-century bronze bowl shows a mounted Mamluk heavy cavalryman. He appears to be wearing a lamellar cuirass, a type of armour which was made from small iron plates laced together. Above his head he holds a slightly curved sabre.

Border of crowns

KING ON A TILE
Medieval churches were often decorated with patterned ceramic tiles. These examples come from Chertsey Abbey, England. They bear a portrait of Richard I, known as Richard Lionheart, who was king of England from 1189 to 1199, and was one of the leaders of the Third Crusade of 1190.

Mamluk cavalryman

Arabic inscription

A SARACEN
Many Saracens used fast horses and shot arrows at the crusaders from their recurved composite bows. Some wore forms of plate armour but many wore mail or padded defences. Round shields were common and curved slashing sabres became popular in the 12th century.

TURKISH WARRIOR
This Italian dish of about 1520 shows a Turkish warrior. The crusades died out in the early 14th century and the great fortified city of Constantinople (now Istanbul) stood between Turkey and the mainland of Europe. However, the city never fully recovered from the damage it suffered during the Fourth Crusade in 1204. In 1453 it finally fell to the Sultan Suleyman the Magnificent. It has remained part of Turkey ever since.

FIGHTING FOR THE FAITH
This mid 13th-century picture shows Christians and Muslims clashing in 1218 during the Christian siege of Damietta at the mouth of the Nile in Egypt. The artist has dressed the Muslims, on the right, rather like Christians.

STRONGHOLDS IN THE EAST
As in the West, the crusaders built stone castles and borrowed some ideas from examples in the East. Crusader castles were built on strong natural sites when possible. This huge castle, Krak des Chevaliers in Syria, was held by the Knights Hospitallers. An outer ring of walls was added in the 13th century.

CROSS-LEGGED KNIGHT
This effigy, carved in the late 13th century, was said to be that of English knight Sir John Holcombe, who died of wounds during the Second Crusade (1147-49). The cross-legged pose is popularly thought to indicate a crusader. In fact it is simply a style used by the sculptors of the time.

Knights of Christ

In 1118 a band of knights who protected Christian pilgrims in the Holy Land were given quarters near the Temple of Jerusalem. These men, known as the Knights Templar (of the temple), became a religious order but differed from other monks by remaining warriors and continuing to fight the Muslims. In the same period another order of monks, who had worked with the sick, became a military order called the Knights of St. John or Knights Hospitaller. When the Christians lost control of the Holy Land in 1291 the Templars, by now less active, found that the European rulers who had supported them did not like their power and their lack of action, and they were disbanded. The Hospitallers moved their base to the Mediterranean and continued fighting the Muslims. The Teutonic Knights, a German order that had become military in 1198, moved to eastern Europe and fought to convert the Slavs to Christianity.

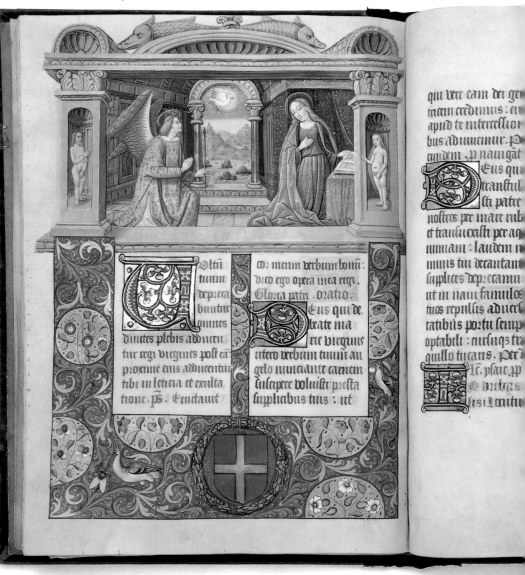

Position of original spout

MEDICINE JAR
The Hospitallers used jars made from decorated pottery called Majolica to hold their medicines. Although a military order, these monks had been caring for the sick since the 11th century and continued to do so while also providing fighting men for the Christian wars against the Muslims.

THE HOSPITAL
Malta was the final home of the Knights of St. John. This engraving of 1586 shows them at work on the great ward of their hospital in the Maltese capital, Valetta.

BRONZE MORTAR
Ingredients for Hospitaller medicines were ground by a pestle in this mortar dating from the 12th or 13th century.

BURNING THE TEMPLARS

After the Christians took control of the Holy Land, the Templars became very rich and powerful, which made them unpopular. King Philip IV of France decided to seize their wealth. The Grand Master, Jacques de Morlay, was burned in 1313 and the Order was suppressed in Europe.

THE FIGHT GOES ON

After the loss of the Holy Land in 1291, the Hospitallers moved first to Cyprus, then in 1310 to Rhodes where they again clashed with the Muslims. This continual struggle meant that despite their wealth, they managed to escape the fate of the Templars.

MASTER AND SERV[...]

A small lacquered [...] decorated with a pi[...] kneeling before a sa[...] needed servants to [...] look after their equi[...] western knights. A [...] life-and-death pow[...] and over the farmer[...] land and provided [...]

GRAND MASTER'S SEAL

A Grand Master led each military order. This seal belonged to Raymond de Berenger, who ruled the Hospitallers from 1363–1374.

PROCESSIONAL CROSS

This early 16th-century cross is made of oak covered with silver plate. The figure of Christ is older. The Evangelists are pictured on the arms of the cross. The cross belonged to the Hospitallers and the coat-of-arms is that of Pierre Decluys, Grand Prior of France from 1522–1535. Each military order had priories or commanderies in several countries which raised money and recruits.

ORDER OF SERVICE *above*

The Knights of St. John were expected to attend church services and to know their Bible in the same way as other monks. Breviaries like this one contained the daily service. The religious knights had to obey strict rules, which were usually based on those of the regular monastic orders. Hospitallers followed the rule of St. Benedict, the Templars that of the Cistercian Order.

THE ART OF SWORDSM[...]

In this section from a 1[...] picture by Kunisada, a [...] called Minamoto Yoshi[...] instructed in swordplay[...] creatures called Tengu. [...] use the sword correctly [...] years of hard work – th[...] many moves that the s[...] had to perfect. Japanes[...] had extremely sharp cu[...]

KNIGHT TEMPLAR

Templars wore a white surcoat with a red cross. This 12th-century fresco from the Templar church at Cressac in France shows a knight galloping into battle.

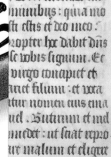

This 19th-centur[...] shows a samurai [...] armour. This is [...] plates of iron, un[...] small laced [...] armour he we[...] jinbaori. He ca[...] swords but also[...] of bamboo and[...] together and b[...] helmet cr[...]

THE RHODES MISSAL

Joining the Knights Hospitaller meant being a skilled fighting man yet rejecting the world for a monastic life. Like other monks, the knights swore to serve the order faithfully, to renounce women, and to help those in need. It is thought that many knights took their vows on this book, the late 15th-century Rhodes Missal.

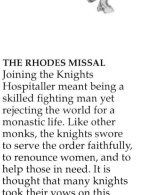

WATER BOTTLE

A water supply was vital in the heat of the Mediterranean and along pilgrim routes in the Holy Land. This metal water bottle of about 1500 bears the cross of the Order of St. John.

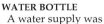

Knig

E**UROPE** v
develope
Europe, a
western e
serving a
1180-1185
military l
Shogun's
by daimy

The professionals

I**N THE HEAT OF BATTLE** even heavily armed squadrons of knights could not break the disciplined ranks of infantry. The wars between France and Burgundy in 1476–1477 showed how mounted knights were unable to defeat solid bodies of pikemen backed up by soldiers using handguns. So by 1500 the infantry was becoming the most important part of any army. In Germany foot soldiers called Landsknechts copied their Swiss neighbours in using pikes and guns. The way men were hired was also changing. Feudal forces, who fought in return for their land, were increasingly being replaced by paid permanent forces of well-trained soldiers backed up by mercenaries and men recruited locally. Although mounted knights still played their part, they were becoming less effective on the battlefield.

PUFFED AND SLASHED ARMOUR
In the late 15th and early 16th centuries the Swiss and German Landsknechts enjoyed showing off by wearing extravagant clothing in the "puffed and slashed" style. This German armour made in about 1520 mimics that style. The slashings are etched and gilt, whereas the surfaces in between are etched to suggest damask or cut velvet cloth.

Bellows visor

Later mail

Steel strips to guard inside of elbow

Puffed and slashed decoration

HANDGUNNERS
Swiss handgunners of the late 15th century fire matchlock guns at enemy soldiers, backed up by wheeled cannon. Already Swiss armies consisted largely of infantry pike formations supported by units of handgunners and cannon.

TWO-HANDED SWORD
Swords like this were useful for cutting the points off pikes carried by enemy soldiers. The lugs on the blade helped prevent an enemy weapon sliding up to the hands. The leather covering the ricasso or blunted section on the blade allowed a shorter grip on the weapon. This example dates to about 1600, by which time these were becoming ceremonial weapons.

Grip covered in wood and leather

Crossguard

Lug

Ricasso with leather covering

Flamboyant or wavy edge

CAT-GUTTER
This German Landsknecht of about 1520 wears partial armour with puffed and slashed breeches and a "bishop's mantle" of mail to guard his neck. As well as a two-handed sword he carries a distinctive short sword that was called a *Katzbalger* (Cat-gutter).

EARLY ARMOU
This 19th-centu
in the great arr
attached to the
cuirass is made
together with si
samurai who w
basically mount

Tempered

IN BLACK AND WHITE

Infantrymen who could afford some protection often chose a half armour without leg pieces to make walking easier. Light horsemen wore similar armour. The open helmet, called a burgonet, let more air get to the face. The black and white effect on this armour of about 1550 was made by leaving some areas as bright steel while painting other parts black. The paint was also thought to protect against rust.

HALBERD

The heavy axehead on this infantry staff weapon could be used to maim an enemy, while the beak on the back could trip up horses or hook a knight from the saddle. This German example dates to about 1500.

Cheek-piece of burgonet

PIKEMAN

This Landsknecht of the 16th century wears the usual elaborate costume and armour, this time surmounted by a plume. As well as his sword he carries a pike similar to the one shown on the right.

Gauntlet

GERMAN CROSSBOW

This crossbow of about 1520 has a bow made from cane and whalebone covered with parchment. When the short crossbow bolt struck armour squarely it could punch through it. Unlike longbows, which needed constant practice, crossbows were spanned mechanically (pp. 50–51) and could be used more easily. They were popular on the European mainland.

Steel stirrup

Cord and plaited leather binding

Tasset

Bowstring of twisted cord

GUN BATTERY

A gunner lowers a glowing linstock to the touchhole of a cannon, from a woodcut of about 1520. The barrels have moulded decoration. The increasing use of cannon was one factor in the decline of the castle and the rise of the heavily-gunned fortress. Field guns were used against enemy cavalry and infantry.

The decline of chivalry

RULERS INCREASINGLY PREFERRED to use professional soldiers, leaving knights to live on their estates. By the 17th century, warfare was becoming more and more the job of full-time soldiers, mercenaries, and middle-class troops. Knights occasionally fought as officers, usually of cavalry, but the medieval fighting man was now only a memory. No longer was knighthood only granted to sons of knights. It was becoming an honour, a title given to people that the monarch thought deserved recognition. This idea still continues in many places, but the knight of old was not forgotten. His image survived, helped partly by old castles and stories of heroes such as King Arthur, and the magic, woven by medieval poets and 19th-century romantics, lives on.

PROCESSIONAL PARTIZAN
With firearms taking over the battlefield many edged weapons were made for ceremonial use only, like this German partizan of about 1690.

Long tasset

Grip

Detachable knee-piece

Butt could be used as a club

CUIRASSIER
The last armoured knights wore armour like this and were known as cuirassiers. The use of massed pikemen and firearms meant that knights could no longer use lances to charge home. Because of the increasing use of guns the armour plates were thickened, making them heavier, so the lower leg defences were left off and replaced with leather riding boots. Unlike this fine etched and gilt Italian example of the early 17th century, many such armours were crudely made.

OLD VERSUS NEW *right*
This engraving of 1632 shows how an armoured cuirassier with a lance could be stopped by an infantryman with a musket. Notice the wheel-lock pistol, a more effective weapon for the horseman, hanging in its holster from the saddle.

PREPARING TO FIRE *left*
An early 17th-century Dutch musketeer pours a measured amount of gunpowder from his powder flask into his musket.

BUFF COAT
Light cavalrymen found that a coat of buff leather was able to stop a sword cut and was more comfortable than full armour. It was worn either alone or with a breastplate and backplate. At this time, breastplates were usually "proofed" or tested by firing a gun at them before they were worn.

Piece of rock which strikes metal to make a spark; this lights the gunpowder and fires the gun

DON QUIXOTE
The Spanish writer Miguel de Cervantes wrote the novel *Don Quixote* in around 1590. The book tells of a foolish old man who jousts with windmills thinking they are giants and treats a peasant girl as his lady, a sad yearning for lost knightly ideals and chivalry.

WHEEL-LOCK PISTOL
With better quality gunpowder and larger numbers of soldiers being armed with guns, there was little place for the armoured knight. Cuirassiers and light cavalry carried two wheel-lock pistols. This German example of about 1590 has an ebony stock inlaid with engraved panels and strips of staghorn.

Ramrod

Key cylinder

Screwdriver

Swivel-eye for suspension

Pivoting pricker to unblock vent

KEY
This German spanner of about 1620 wound up a spring on the wheel-lock which, when released by the sear, or trigger, spanned a wheel and lowered the cock against it, causing a shower of sparks to fire the gunpowder.

This late 16th-century cartridge-box was designed to hang from a belt

THE VICTOR
The chivalrous ideal knight is shown about to receive his prize on this Victorian silhouette. The knight in shining armour, the quest for the Holy Grail, and other legendary Arthurian adventures appealed to the romantic Victorian mind.

Index

Acknowledgments

Dorling Kindersley would like to thank:
The Wallace Collection, the Royal Armouries, the British Museum, and the Museum of the Order of St. John for providing items for photography; English Heritage, the National Trust, and Cadw (Welsh Historical Monuments), for permission to photograph at Rochester, Bodiam, and Caerphilly Castles; David Edge of the Wallace Collection; Paul Cannings, Jonathan Waller, John Waller, Bob Dow, Ray Monery, and Julia Harris for acting as models; Anita Burger for make-up; Joanna Cameron for illustrations (pages 22-23); Angels and Burmans for costumes; Sharon Spencer and Manisha Patel for design assistance; Helena Spiteri for editorial assistance; Céline Carez for research.

Picture credits

t=top, b=bottom, c=centre, l=left, r=right

Ancient Art & Architecture Collection: 58cl, 58c. 58tr, 59bl
Bridgeman Art Library: 53b; 54c; /Biblioteca Estense, Modena: 10b; /British Library: 19tc, 20tr, 20c, 38cr, 39c, 49tr, 54tl; /Bibliotheque Municipal de Lyon: 55c; /Bibliotheque Nationale, Paris: 11br, 15tr, 22cr, 25tl, 41tr, 42bl, 43t, 54bl, 57tr; /Corpus Christi College, Cambridge: 13rc; /Corpus Christi College, Oxford: 54br; /Giraudon/Musee Conde, Chantilly: 50bl; /51bl; /Vatican Library, Rome: 50br; /Victoria & Albert Museum 37cl; /Wrangham Collection: 59c
Burgerbibliothek, Bern: 25rc
Christ Church, Oxford/Photo: Bodleian Library:27tl
E.T. Archive: 6bl, 11tl, 18bl, 27tr, 30bl, 31bl, 33cl, 33cr, 39tr, 41c, 49bl, 57bc, 58cr, 59cl, 60c; /Btitish Library:19bc, 32c; /British Museum:27bl; /Fitzwilliam Museum, Cambridge: 48rc
Robert Harding Picture Library: 8tl, 12rc, 18tr, 22bl, 26c, 34br, 34bl, 55bl; /British Library: 11lc, 34cl, 44b, 45bl
Michael Holford: 8bl, 9tr, 52c, 55br
Hulton-Deutsch Collection: 56cl
A.F. Kersting: 9cl
Mansell Collection: 11bl, 21lc, 39tr, 46br, 55tl, 63bl, /Alinari: 46tr
Bildarchiv Foto Marburg: 48br
Arxiu Mas: 54cl
Stadtbibliothek Nurnberg: 17rc
Osterreichische Nationalbibliotehek, Vienna, (Cod.2597, f.15): 40br
Pierpont Morgan Library, New York: 29c
Scala: 7br, 33t, 34tlc. 36cl
Stiftsbibliothek St Gallen: 6c
Syndication International: 26br, 27cl, 27tcl, 32bc, 37tl, 41tl, 50tr, 53l, 57tl; /Photo. Trevor Wood: 36tr
Courtesy of the Board of Trustees of the Victoria & Albert Museum: 54b.

Every effort has been made to trace the copyright holders and we apologise in advance for for any unintentional omissions. We would be pleased to insert the appropriate acknowledgment in any subsequent edition of this publication.

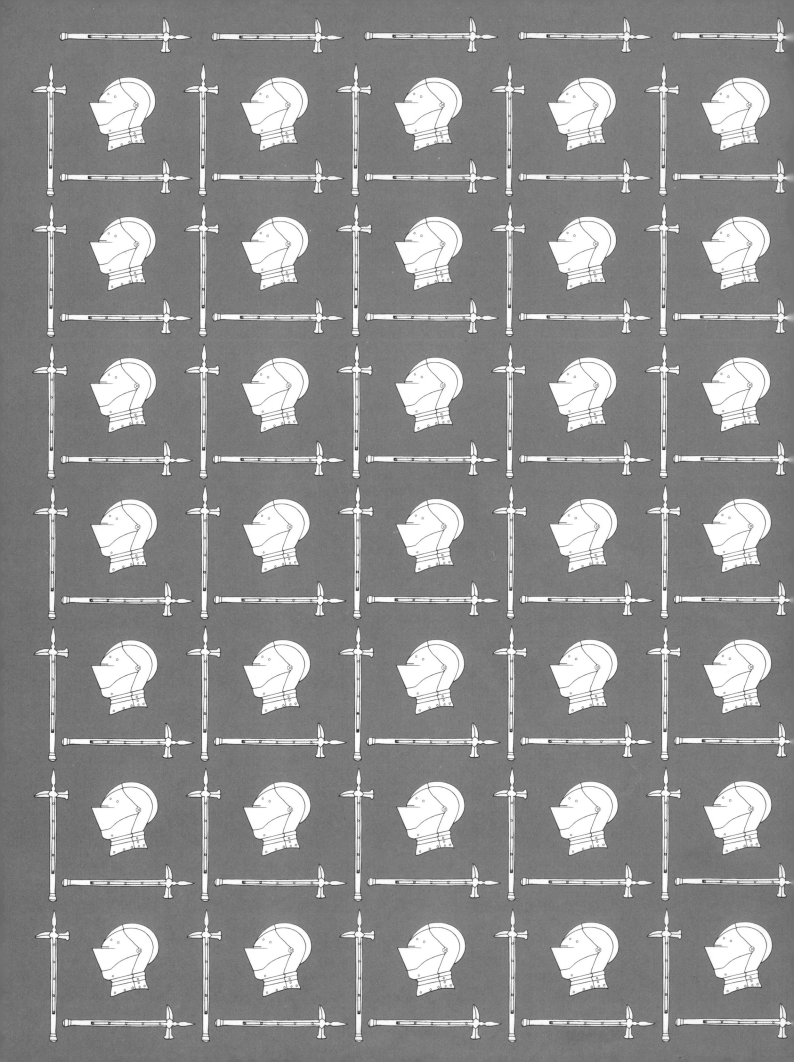